BIG IDEAS IN BRIEF

BIG IDEAS IN BRIEF

IAN CROFTON

Quercus

CONTENTS

Introduction

What makes a big idea big? In 1953 the British philosopher Isaiah Berlin published a famous essay entitled *The Hedgehog and the Fox*, based on a fragment from a lost fable by the ancient Greek poet Archilochus: 'The fox knows many little things, but the hedgehog knows one big thing.'

Berlin used this little fable as the basis for dividing the world's great thinkers and writers into two categories, the foxes and the hedgehogs. A hedgehog has one big idea, and sees the world entirely through this single lens. Berlin cites a number of examples of hedgehogs, including the philosophers Plato, Hegel and Nietzsche, and the writers Dante, Dostoevsky, Ibsen and Proust. In contrast foxes – including Aristotle, Shakespeare, Montaigne and Goethe – draw on a wide range of ideas and experiences, and view the world from a variety of perspectives.

The present book includes a number of big 'hedgehog' ideas – Plato's Forms, Hegel's idealism, Marx's dialectical materialism, to name but a few. But its broad scope, its willingness to include many mutually contradictory concepts, its questioning of assumptions, all make it very much a foxy sort of enterprise.

Although drawing on a range of academic disciplines, this small book makes no claims to comprehensiveness. Rather, it selects a number of ideas that general readers may feel they ought to know a little about, and gives them a succinct summary of the key points. By far the longest sections are devoted to philosophical and political ideas, for which no apology is made, but the reader will also find a range of topics drawn from religion, science, economics, sociology, anthropology, psychology and the arts. For those wanting a fuller treatment of scientific ideas, there is an entire volume in the same series devoted to that subject.

Ian Crofton
May 2011

Philosophy

The term 'philosophy' comes from the ancient Greek word *philosophos*, meaning 'lover of wisdom', and for the ancient Greeks philosophy had a very wide scope. Today, we take a narrower view as to what constitutes philosophy, an activity which has been defined as the critical examination of the basis for fundamental beliefs as to what is true, and the analysis of the concepts we use in expressing such beliefs.

The Greek philosophers before Socrates (c.469–399 BC) were predominantly concerned with speculations regarding the physical world, such as the nature of matter or the shape of the universe. Such inquiries became known in the Middle Ages as 'natural philosophy' – what we now call science.

Science can be classified as a 'first-order' activity, concerned with discovering the truth about the physical world. Another first-order activity is moralizing – telling us what actions are good and which are bad. Philosophy, in contrast, is a 'second-order' activity, one that examines the assumptions lying behind first-order activities.

Socrates – whose thinking is only preserved through dialogues written down by his pupil Plato (see page 12) – turned the focus of philosophy onto questions involving humanity, such as 'What is good?' This was the beginning of ethics, the branch of philosophy that seeks to clarify the basis of moral judgements. Socrates also developed methods of testing the validity of arguments – the beginnings of logic.

Ethics and logic are two of the major branches of philosophy. A third major branch, metaphysics, asks questions about the ultimate nature of reality, such as 'What is being?' Other fields within philosophy include epistemology, which studies the nature of knowledge; and aesthetics, which examines the nature of beauty and art, and questions the basis of critical judgements.

In addition, there are philosophies of a wide range of other first-order subjects, such as science, history, and political theory.

Reason

Reason is a word with a variety of shades of meaning. It is the human faculty that enables us to make logical inferences, arguing from the general to the particular (deduction) or from the particular to the general (induction). For some philosophers, 'reason' denotes the intellect regarded as a source of knowledge, as opposed to experience.

Reason is often contrasted with emotion or imagination or insanity or faith. In the 13th century, St Thomas Aquinas sought to reconcile faith and reason, giving the latter a place in Christian theology.

In the 18th century, thinkers of the Enlightenment emphasized the primacy of reason, seeking to abolish superstition and intolerance, and to reform the public sphere on rational lines. In reaction, the Romantic movement that arose towards the end of the 18th century emphasized the centrality of individual feeling in human experience (see page 386).

This depiction of Newton by the English romantic William Blake's depicts a figure obsessed with reason and oblivious to the natural world around him — yet it also mirrors the depiction of God in *The Ancient of Days* (page 141).

Platonism

The whole of Western philosophy has been described as 'a series of footnotes to Plato' – such has been the enduring influence of the ancient Greek philosopher.

Plato (c.427–347 BC) lived and taught in Athens, where he set up a school of philosophy known as the Academy. He was a pupil of Socrates (see pages 8–9), and most of his writings are written in the form of dialogues between Socrates and his followers. It is unknown how closely these represent Socrates' own thought, as opposed to that of Plato himself.

The dialogues employ what is known as the 'Socratic method', in which Socrates pretends ignorance and asks a follower questions, leading them on until they contradict themselves. In this way, issues are clarified, and a closer approach is made to the truth. The early dialogues are concerned with 'virtues' such as piety and courage, and appear to conclude that virtue is knowledge, and that wrongdoing is the result of ignorance. Of particular significance is the method itself, involving the rigorous challenging of assumptions and an insistence upon logical argument – the hallmarks of true philosophy.

The dialogues also discuss the ultimate nature of reality. For Plato this consists of Forms, or Ideas, rather than what we experience in the material world. The supreme Form is the good, which equates to knowledge. To illustrate this concept, in *The Republic* Plato presents the fable of the prisoners in the cave (see page 14). *The Republic* is also concerned with politics, discussing the nature of justice and imagining an ideal, just state ruled by philosopher-kings.

Under the later Roman empire, the Neo-Platonists developed a mystical philosophy based on Plato's Forms, and came up with a hierarchy of increasingly esoteric knowledge that they called the chain of being. This was influential among Jewish, Christian and Islamic philosophers down to the Renaissance and beyond, but has not proved as important as the works of Plato himself.

Plato's cave

In *The Republic*, Plato presents a fable in which humanity is likened to prisoners chained in a cave. All they can see is the wall in front of them, and thus their only experience of objects is the shadows cast on the wall by a fire. According to Plato, this is analogous to our ignorance of ultimate reality, which consists of idealized and unchangeable Forms.

Thus a table is but an imperfect copy or shadow of an ideal table; a horse is just a manifestation of an archetype of horsiness. As individual horses are all different in some ways, none represent the real, ideal horse. The objects in the world we experience are forever changing: tables were once trees; horses are born, grow and die. True knowledge is only attainable in the unobservable world of Forms; all that we take as knowledge in the world of the senses is in fact nothing more than opinion or belief.

Aristotelianism

The Greek philosopher Aristotle (384–322 BC) was a pupil of Plato, but his approach was very different. Whereas Plato held that ultimate reality was beyond human experience, Aristotle was concerned with studying the world as he found it. He wrote on a wide range of subjects, from logic, ethics, aesthetics and politics to physics, metaphysics, astronomy, meteorology, psychology, biology and zoology.

Contrary to Plato, Aristotle held that reality is made up of individual substances, not abstract entities. For him, the only source of knowledge is the evidence supplied by our senses, and he asserted that through the use of reason we can establish the distinctive qualities of things – in other words, their essences. Thus from the particular we can infer the general.

Aristotle sought to place such reasoning on a sound basis, and explored the nature of the syllogism (see page 88), a method of inference of which the following is an example: 'All Greeks are human; all humans are mortal; therefore all Greeks are mortal.' In showing what kinds of inference were valid, and which were not, Aristotle established the basis of formal logic, and gave a logical foundation to science.

In analysing poetry and drama, Aristotle held that art embodies nature in an idealized form, that the essence of beauty is symmetry and order, and that the function of tragedy is to purge the emotions through pity and terror. He argued that it is important for our happiness to exercise reason, the essential human capacity. Exercising reason involves both intellectual endeavour and the control of one's emotions to achieve a 'golden mean' between austerity and excess (see page 106).

During the European Dark Ages, Aristotle's teachings were preserved by scholars in the Islamic world. When from the 12th century Latin translations began to appear in Europe, they had a profound impact, providing a framework for the subsequent development of Western thought.

Humanism

Humanism can broadly be defined as an intellectual attitude that puts human beings at the centre of our concerns. The Greek philosophers before Socrates were primarily concerned with the nature of the universe, whereas Socrates, Plato and Aristotle, with their interest in politics and ethics, placed humans at centre stage.

In the European Middle Ages, intellectual effort was largely concerned with God and theology. But during the Renaissance there was a revival of interest in the writings of the ancient Greeks and Romans, which were largely secular in approach. Art, literature and scholarship all began to place the focus more firmly on human beings, although the existence or supremacy of God was rarely denied. With the beginning of the Scientific Revolution in the 16th century, people began to believe that human reason could fathom the workings of the universe. Today, the term 'humanism' often implies atheism, or at least a strongly secular attitude.

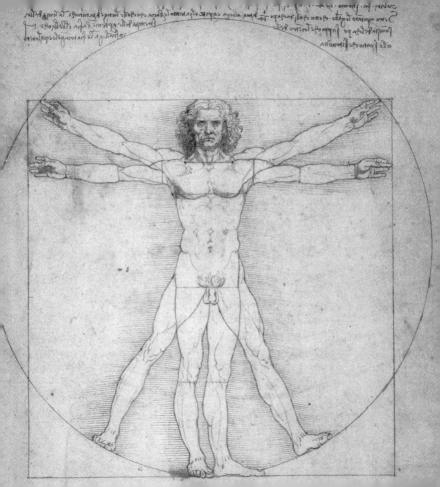

Human nature

The question as to whether there is such a thing as 'human nature' – and if so, what that nature is – has vexed thinkers for many centuries. Christian doctrine holds that since the Fall – when Adam and Eve were expelled from the Garden of Eden for disobeying God – every human is born into 'original sin'. According to this view, all humans are innately sinful, and salvation is only possible through various combinations (depending on the denomination) of priestly mediation, good works and, overridingly, faith (see page 142).

English philosopher Thomas Hobbes (1588–1679) took a similarly dim view of human nature, arguing that the life of early man was 'nasty, brutish and short'. He held that only a strictly ordered society led by a ruler wielding absolute power could keep people from 'continual fear and danger of violent death'.

To this day, political conservatives tend to emphasize the importance of authority and hierarchy, and dismiss attempts to improve the lot of the poor as 'social engineering' doomed to failure, owing to their perception of humans as being by nature lazy and selfish.

In the 18th century, the French philosopher Jean-Jacques Rousseau (1712–78) took the opposite view of human nature, arguing that humans in a state of nature are 'noble savages', their natural goodness only corrupted by society.

A generation after Hobbes, another English philosopher, John Locke (see page 71), denied that there was any such thing as human nature, claiming that humans were born as 'blank slates'. Humans, Locke maintained, can thus be moulded by their environment and upbringing, and Locke placed great emphasis on the importance of education.

Political thinkers of the left – socialists, communists and anarchists – have generally adopted this position, believing that if society is ordered in the right way, humans will behave well, cooperate with each other selflessly and achieve happiness. This is the political aspect of the nature vs nurture debate (see page 198).

Love

Today, when we hear the word 'love' the first thing that we tend to think of is the yearning and passionate desire of one person for another – 'romantic' love. Some feminists dismiss this as no more than a cultural construct to reinforce male domination, while social biologists assert that its function is evolutionary, related to sexual selection.

The ancient Greeks distinguished three types of love: affection (*philos*), as between friend and friend; sexual love (*eros*); and selfless love (*agape*). *Agape* is the word used in the original Greek of St Paul (1 Corinthians 13:13) – 'And now these three remain: faith, hope and love. But the greatest of these is love.' In Christian theology, the love of God for his creation – in Dante's words, 'The love that moves the sun and the other stars' – is the ultimate love. Plato and Aristotle considered love to be a yearning for perfection: 'platonic love' is beyond physical desire, and the ultimate love is the love of wisdom – the original meaning of the word 'philosophy'.

History

At its simplest, history comprises the stories we tell ourselves about the past. The earliest historical writings were king lists, such as those found in the ancient Middle East. These usually traced the lineage of the ruling monarch back to a god, thereby giving divine sanction to his right to rule. Myths and legends elaborated on such lineages, explaining how things in the world came to be as they are.

Later, when writers began to record the more recent past, they tended to slant their narratives to show off their own country, culture or religion in the best light – just as myths and legends had done. The tendency for historians to write with ulterior motives has been a recurring trend.

In the 19th century, for example, many historians wrote history as an account of human progress, culminating in what they regarded as the superiority of the state of affairs pertaining in their own day. For some British historians such as Lord

Macaulay (1800–59), history was the irresistible march towards constitutional monarchy and parliamentary democracy. In Germany, the philosopher G.W.F. Hegel (see page 63) saw history as an inevitable unfolding of abstract ideas, culminating in the absolutist Prussian state under which he lived. Marx took a similarly deterministic approach, but for him the goal of history was perfect communism (see pages 258–261).

Historians today reject the idea that history is the working out of some overarching purpose, and strive towards more objective accounts. And yet complete objectivity is not attainable in history. Even if a fact can be demonstrated to be irrefutably true, history consists of a selection of facts marshalled into some kind of account or explanation, and in the very act of deciding which facts are important, and how they relate to other facts, the historian will inevitably betray the perspective of his or her own class, culture and even gender.

Nature

Nature is one of those words, like 'love', that carry a multiplicity of meanings and a huge amount of cultural baggage. The 'nature' of something can mean its essence, or defining quality (see, for example, human nature, page 20). 'Nature' can also denote the entirety of the physical universe, contrasted with the world of ideas (see, for example, Plato's Forms, page 14) or spirituality.

Alternatively, 'nature' can suggest all that is separate from 'civilization'. For much of human history, nature in this sense was regarded as abhorrent. Mountains and forests, for example, were dangerous, useless and therefore ugly. Only landscapes tamed by cultivation and industry had moral or aesthetic value. But beginning in the later 18th century the Romantic movement (see page 386) altered our perspective, portraying wild places as sources of sublime inspiration. More recently, the environmental movement has emphasized the ecological value of untouched wilderness (see page 268).

George Stubbs's painting *A Horse Affrighted by a Lion* (1777) depicts nature in both its brutal and Romantic aspects.

Metaphysics

Metaphysics is the branch of philosophy concerned with being, knowing and the ultimate nature of reality. It addresses questions of the existence or otherwise of God and of the external world, the nature of time and space, the relation of mind to body, the reality or otherwise of causation, and the respective claims of determinism and free will in human affairs. The aspect of metaphysics concerned with knowing is termed epistemology (see page 54).

Metaphysical questions dominated philosophical inquiry from the time of the ancient Greeks through to the Middle Ages and beyond. Plato, for example, held that reality only exists in the abstract world of Forms (see page 14), while 13th-century Christian theologian St Thomas Aquinas used Aristotelian reasoning to establish the existence of God.

In the 17th century, the French philosopher René Descartes concluded through rational argument that mind and body are two separate entities, and was then obliged to speculate as to how the immaterial and the material could interact (see page 43).

The claims made by metaphysicians regarding realities beyond our power of observation or even reason have led many to sneer that these dreamers live entirely in cloud-cuckoo-land. In the 18th century the Scottish philosopher David Hume proposed two questions that should be asked of a work of metaphysics. Firstly, 'Does it contain any abstract reasoning concerning quantity or number?' Secondly, 'Does it contain any experimental reasoning, concerning matter of fact and existence?' If the answer to both was 'No', Hume's advice was to throw the book in the fire, 'for it can contain nothing but sophistry and illusion'.

In the early 20th century logical positivist thinkers (see page 80) attacked metaphysics on similar grounds, while others suggested that the tangles that metaphysicians involved themselves in arose out of misconceptions about the way that language works. However, despite these critiques, metaphysical questions continue to occupy the minds of many philosophers.

Purpose

The belief that life, the universe and everything has a purpose – or 'final cause' – is called teleology. This intellectual tendency may arise out of the way that humans behave, generally acting rationally to achieve particular goals. The sorts of language we use to describe our aim-oriented behaviour encourages us to apply this sort of language – involving preordained or anticipated ends – to non-human processes.

Implicit or explicit in much teleological thinking is the concept of a design lying behind natural phenomena, especially life on Earth. Some Christians insist that this would not be possible without an 'intelligent designer', i.e. God. The language-habit of assigning purpose to things is a trap that even committed Darwinists sometimes make, but it is really a shorthand way of describing how a random genetic mutation may by chance provide a functional advantage to an organism and so be perpetuated by natural selection (see page 196).

The absurd

During the course of the 19th century, the certainty of many people that the world was ordained by God began to be eroded. First of all, the geologists established that the Earth must be very much older than suggested in the biblical account. They also showed, via fossils, that many creatures had once lived on Earth that were now extinct.

Then Charles Darwin (1809–82) showed how living creatures evolved via natural selection (see page 196), rather than being instantaneously created in their present forms by God. Many thinking people found Darwin's arguments irrefutable, and the implications terrifying. The German philosopher Friedrich Nietzsche voiced the fears of many when in 1882 he declared 'God is dead.'

If God was not responsible for life, then life was left without a divine purpose, or perhaps without any purpose at all. The general human inclination to seek meaning in existence was thwarted by the bald facts of science. Humans could no longer answer the perennial question, 'Why are we here?'

This conflict resulted in the apprehension that the universe is meaningless and irrational – absurd. Humanity appeared to face a crisis. The question of how to act in such an absurd universe is one of the main concerns of the philosophical movement known as existentialism (see page 36).

Although existentialism and the notion of the absurd have their roots in the 19th century, they took a particular hold on the Western mind in the aftermath of the Second World War. The Holocaust had shown just how inhuman humans could be, and the dropping of the atom bombs on Hiroshima and Nagasaki presented a vision of how humanity might annihilate itself entirely. The resulting sense of hopelessness, anxiety and bewilderment gave rise to an 'absurdist' tendency in literature, epitomized by Samuel Beckett's play *Waiting for Godot* (1953) – in which two characters wait endlessly for a third, the suggestively named Godot, who never arrives.

Being

The study of being is called ontology. Its primary concern is with which things exist and which do not. Such things include universals, minds independent of bodies, things independent of the mind, free will, essences and God.

If the thing in question is held to exist, then the question arises as to whether it exists independently of minds or language. It may also be asked whether it is irreducible, or is made up of other constituents. Questions may also be posed as to whether such things exist as substances, or as qualities, or as properties, or as relations to other things.

One of the most enduring debates in philosophy regards the status of universals – general terms such as 'blue' or 'cat'. 'Realists' hold that universals exist independently of the mind, while at the other end of the spectrum, extreme 'nominalists' argue that the objects of such general terms have nothing in common except the general term itself.

To be is to do

— Socrates

To do is to be

— Sartre

Do Be Do Be Do

— Sinatra

Existentialism

Existentialism is a trend in philosophy that asks in broad terms how the individual should act in an 'absurd' universe without meaning, purpose, rationality or morality (see page 32). In such a universe, an individual's existence consists of complete freedom to choose.

The individual's choices must be unconstrained by references to generalizations and abstractions such as human nature, scientific or historical determinism, morality or rationality. But they must be made in full recognition of the existence of other individuals and objects. 'Authenticity' resides in accepting this absolute freedom, while to deny it is 'bad faith'. The individual is continually confronted with choices, and must take complete responsibility for his or her actions, giving rise to a condition of *angst* or anxiety.

Existentialism has been particularly influential in continental Europe. One of the first recognizably existential thinkers was the Danish philosopher Søren Kierkegaard (1813–55). A Christian, he emphasized the importance of personal choice and commitment, and asserted that in the face of the absurd one is free to choose to believe – to make a 'leap of faith'.

Another thinker who influenced later existentialists was the German philosopher Friedrich Nietzsche (1844–1900). Dismissing the claims of religion, science, metaphysics or rationality to have established either absolute truth or absolute values, he asserted that in a world without structure or purpose the individual must reject the 'slave morality' of Christianity and aspire towards new values, 'beyond good and evil'. The exceptional individual must adopt the 'will to power', and enhance life through creativity.

In the 20th century, one of the leading exponents of existentialism was the German philosopher Martin Heidegger (1889–1976). He was deeply concerned with the 'meaning of being', and was responsible for the concepts of authenticity and *angst*. In France, the leading proponent was the novelist, playwright and philosopher Jean-Paul Sartre (1905–80), who coined the existentialist term 'bad faith'.

Identity

The problem of determining whether an object or a person has the same identity through time is one that has long vexed philosophers. Imagine an old axe that needs its handle replacing; then, a few years later, its head needs replacing too. When this is done, in what sense if any is it the same old axe?

Similar questions can be asked of human beings. I may still have the same DNA that I had 30 years ago, but nearly all of the cells in my body will have been replaced. Although there is a passing resemblance, I do not look the same. Nor do my opinions or my behaviour resemble those of my younger self. In what sense am I the same person? Maybe, some philosophers conclude, it is mistaken to conceive of a 'substantial self' beyond individual thoughts, memories and experiences. Maybe the self resides in process, not substance.

Consciousness

Consciousness is our awareness not only of the external world, but of ourselves and of what occurs in our own minds. This inner world includes feelings, memories, beliefs, perceptions and other mental events. Some have suggested that consciousness is what distinguishes humans from the other animals. Animals are clearly conscious of the external world, but to what extent they are self-conscious, if at all, is a moot point. They clearly process sensory inputs out of which actions emerge; but observing human behaviour, without the benefit of introspection, we could say no more of humans.

One of the great challenges of contemporary neuroscience is to find a material basis for consciousness. The functions of different parts of the brain are being unravelled, and some physicists have suggested that consciousness may involve quantum events (see page 182). However, consciousness is a subjective experience, so perhaps can never be entirely elucidated by mechanistic explanations.

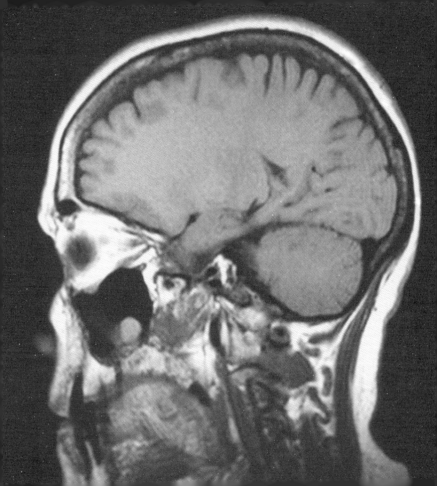

Mind

It is easier to describe the functions of what we call 'mind' than to say what kind of a thing it is. The mind has been defined as the faculty that enables us to perceive, believe, reason, remember, feel and will. Whether the mind is simply the sum of our mental processes – our perceptions, beliefs, reasonings, memories, feelings and decisions – or whether there is something separate about the mind, above and beyond the events that occur within it, is one of those ticklish questions that keep philosophers in business.

Some would suggest that the problem is illusory, resulting from the fact that we have this word 'mind', and therefore assume that because we have a word for it, it must be some kind of real and distinct thing – something with a privileged status, akin to 'soul', perhaps (see page 150).

There are other issues to do with the nature of mind that have exercised philosophers through the ages. Is it the same kind of thing as the body, or different? This is known as the 'mind-body problem'.

Idealists (see page 62) hold that only the realm of ideas is real, and that the body is merely a projection of the mind. In contrast, materialists (see page 64) hold that only the physical world is real, and the mind is merely a function of the body. These are both 'monist' positions; monism (from the Greek *monos*, 'single') holds that reality consists of only one kind of thing.

In contrast to monists, dualists assert that mind and body are two different things. The most famous dualist position is that enunciated by the 17th-century French philosopher René Descartes (see page 68), who held that mind and body are separate substances, and yet still capable of interaction. In the 20th century, this state of affairs was mockingly characterized by British philosopher Gilbert Ryle as 'the ghost in the machine'.

Change and motion

The question as to whether change and motion are real or illusory was first raised by a number of Greek philosophers in the 5th century BC. Parmenides held that reality is single and unchanging. Only being is real; everything is in a permanent state of being, and non-being is illusory. For change or motion to occur, being would have to become non-being, which is contradictory. The information from our senses which suggests that change and motion do occur shows only that our senses mislead us. Zeno of Elea, a follower of Parmenides, devised a number of paradoxes to illustrate these points.

In opposition to this position, Heraclitus held that reality consists of flux (constant change) and motion, and famously asserted, 'You cannot step into the same river twice.' Every object is a 'harmony of opposite tensions', and behind this process lies an organizing principle he called *logos*, analogous to human reason.

Determinism

Determinism is the doctrine that everything that happens has a cause and is therefore inevitable. These effects become in their turn the causes of further effects. Thus chains of cause and effect extend through time and space. For some, they are a manifestation of the will of God, the first cause (see page 48). For others, they are the inevitable consequence of the laws of nature.

In science, the discovery by Isaac Newton of the laws of motion and gravitation (see page 178) provided the basis for an entirely mechanistic explanation of the universe. This led the French astronomer Pierre-Simon Laplace (1749–1827) to assert that it was possible for the mind – if provided with data regarding all the forces operating in the universe, together with information about the mass, dimensions and positions of all the objects that lie within it – to work out both the past and the future of everything.

But already by Laplace's time doubts had been cast. The 18th-century Scottish philosopher David Hume suggested that causality may be no more than a habit of mind, without any logical validity (see page 72). And in the 20th century, quantum mechanics has shown that in the realm of subatomic particles, indeterminacy prevails (see page 183).

The fact that determinism appears to deny the existence of free will (see page 50), and therefore the moral responsibility of individuals for their actions, presents a central problem in ethics. In Christian theology, the doctrine of predestination (see page 160) asserts that certain individuals are destined for salvation and others to damnation, however they behave.

In politics, those on the right tend to emphasize the individual's own responsibility for their condition (wealth, health, etc.), while those on the left point out that an individual's condition is to a great extent determined by external factors such as environment, education and upbringing.

First cause

First-cause theories – an aspect of determinism (see page 46) – hold that behind every event lies a cause, which in turn is caused by something else, and so on, extending back in time. Unwilling to accept an infinitely receding chain of cause and effect, these theories assert that there must be a first or original cause.

Aristotle held that the universe has always been in existence, so the 'prime mover' or 'unmoved mover' is that which sustains the universe. He characterized this prime mover as something like pure thought. The medieval theologian St Thomas Aquinas, influenced by Aristotle, developed what is known as the cosmological argument for the existence of God. The universe could not exist without an uncaused first cause, which he asserted must be God. Modern cosmology proposes that the universe began with the Big Bang (see page 188) and dispenses with the need of a transcendent first cause.

Aristotle (right) and
Plato, as depicted
in Raphael's fresco
The School of Athens.

Free will

Free will is the ability of humans to make free choices and so carve out their own destinies – as opposed to the idea that all events, including human actions, have causes and are therefore inevitable. The doctrine of free will would thus appear to be in absolute contradiction to determinism (see page 46), but in fact there has been much debate regarding whether they are completely incompatible or not.

In theology, the notion of free will appears to contradict the concept of an omniscient, omnipotent and benevolent God, and yet the whole concept of sin hinges on the ability of humans to choose between good and evil. In the biblical book of Genesis, God gives Adam and Eve – and by implication all their descendants – the freedom to choose badly and to disobey him. The analogy is often made with loving parents, who as their children grow older give them greater freedom to make their own mistakes and learn from them.

In Christian theology, God's benevolence is embodied in the idea of grace, which is the gift of salvation to sinners, even though that salvation is unmerited. Similarly, the doctrine of predestination (see page 160) attempts to reconcile free will and divine omnipotence, by suggesting that God has decided in advance who will be saved and who will be damned.

The reality of free will seems to be universally assumed in human societies. It underlies the idea that we are each morally responsible for our actions, and underpins all systems of law – although in most legal systems there is a minimum age below which children are held not to be responsible for the crimes they commit.

Some philosophers argue that even if we live in an entirely deterministic universe, humans still universally act as if we really do have free will. The French existentialist Jean-Paul Sartre (see page 37) stated that even if our situations are entirely determined by historical and social forces, we are still 'condemned to be free'.

Dialectic

Dialectic is a method of logical debate in which two opposing views are discussed, not with the idea that one should be declared to be true, but with the aim of resolving the differences between them, and so coming closer to the truth. This is the basis of the Socratic method, as described by Plato (see page 12).

In the modern era, the term came to have a more metaphysical meaning. According to the 'absolute idealism' of the German philosopher G.W.F. Hegel (see page 63), there is no barrier between reality and our knowledge of it. Concepts unfold through history via a succession of contradictions and resolutions: a thesis gives rise to its negation, the antithesis, and out of this tension emerges a new synthesis. In the 'dialectical materialism' of Karl Marx (see page 260), Hegel's idealism is rejected, and history is held to progress through the struggle between the classes, a struggle that is itself determined by blind economic forces.

Socrates (right) engaged in a dialectical debate in *The School of Athens*.

Epistemology

Epistemology, one of the principal branches of modern philosophy, is the study of the nature of knowledge. The ancient Greeks inquired into the differences between knowledge, truth and belief. For Plato, knowledge is concerned with the Forms (see page 14), the ultimate, unchanging reality only apprehensible through the exercise of reason. In contrast, according to Plato, the ever-changing world grasped by the senses is the subject of belief, rather than knowledge.

The Scientific Revolution initiated in the early 16th century by the Polish astronomer Nicolaus Copernicus undercut the teachings of the Bible and the Church, hitherto regarded as the repositories of truth. This gave rise to new approaches to problems of knowledge – for example, the rational scepticism of René Descartes (see page 68), who argued there were no grounds for accepting the evidence of the senses, and concluded that the only certainty was that, because he knew he was thinking, he knew he existed.

In contrast to Descartes, empiricists such as John Locke (see page 71) argued that our ideas derive entirely from our sense impressions. The Scottish philosopher David Hume (see page 71) went further, rejecting the possibility of any knowledge that does not derive from experience. A radical sceptic, he suggested that most of what we take to be true is a matter of psychological habit, and that virtually nothing we think we know about existence can logically be shown to be the case.

The German philosopher Immanuel Kant argued that knowledge, although partially derived from sensory impressions, is dependent on certain basic 'forms' or 'categories' (such as time, space and causality) inherent in the human understanding.

Kant's fellow German, G.W.F. Hegel, argued that there was no distinction between reality and our knowledge of it, a position known as 'absolute idealism' (see page 63). These and a number of other approaches to epistemological problems are discussed in more detail on the following pages.

Truth

If it accords with the facts, the statement 'Your dress is made of silk' is true. The statement 'I like your dress' may also be true, if the speaker is not lying. The first statement embodies an objective truth; it concerns an external phenomenon (an 'object'), and can be shown to be true or false. The second statement embodies a subjective truth, characterizing as it does the feelings, opinion or perception of an individual (a 'subject'). It cannot be shown to be either true or false.

Some philosophers claim there are absolute truths (see, for example, Plato's Forms, page 14), while others maintain that truths can only ever be relative (pragmatism and instrumentalism; see page 78). Some argue that truths can only be arrived at through reasoning from first principles (rationalism; see page 68), while others hold that the only truths are those gained from experience (empiricism; see page 70).

One of Crete's own prophets has said it:

'Cretans are always liars.'

St Paul, Epistle to Titus, 1:12

Imagination

Imagination is the human faculty that allows us to picture things which are not in front of our eyes, and even to conceive of things that do not exist in the external world. In the first case, it overlaps with memory (see page 352); in the second, it is often associated with creativity.

It might be asked in what way, if at all, the things we imagine are real or true. I can imagine a red swan, but such an animal has yet to be observed in the wild. All forms of art (painting, music, poetry and so on) emerge from the imagination. In the artistic context, this might be described as the faculty through which we synthesize new things from our experience of the external world, combined with our knowledge of artistic conventions and traditions. Art consists of actual objects or processes, which people experience with varying degrees of intensity. Both the creation of works of the imagination and their consumption are actual events.

It was the Romantics (see page 386) who declared imagination to be the supreme human faculty, emphasizing the unique and central role of the artist in human affairs. The poet Samuel Taylor Coleridge held the 'primary imagination' to be 'a repetition in the finite mind of the eternal act of creation in the infinite I AM'. His friend William Wordsworth defined imagination as:

> ... absolute power
> And clearest insight, amplitude of mind,
> And reason, in her most exalted mood.

Another Romantic poet, Percy Bysshe Shelley, asserted that imagination is 'the great instrument of moral good' – perhaps identifying imagination with empathy.

Although Wordsworth saw that reason plays a role in imagination, the legacy of Romanticism has largely been to set imagination against reason and/or science. But when one thinks, for example, of Newton's analogy between an apple falling to the ground and the Earth orbiting the Sun, it is clear that some of the most important scientific breakthroughs have come about through leaps of the imagination.

Ideas

The word 'idea' can have a variety of meanings. It can refer to any content of the mind, or the thought or mental representation of a particular thing, or a plan or intention to do something, or the characterization of something in general terms, i.e. a concept or category.

For Plato, reality consisted of immaterial universals that he called Forms or Ideas (see page 14). These were external to the mind, whereas for idealist philosophers (see page 62), there is no external reality separate from the ideas that occur within the mind. Rationalists (see page 68) hold that we are born with certain innate ideas from which all knowledge can be deduced, whereas empiricists (see page 70) reject innate ideas, holding that the mind only acquires ideas through experience of the external world. Instrumentalists (see page 79) hold that ideas are no more than tools for dealing with practical problems.

Idealism

In the philosophical context, the term 'idealism' is applied to any theory that holds that reality does not exist independently of the mind, or that reality can only be known through our own mental categories and constructs. It is a 'monistic' position, holding that reality is made up of only one kind of substance, i.e. mind, as opposed to the 'dualist' position, which states that mind and matter are two different kinds of thing (see page 43).

Idealism is contrasted with materialism, another monist position, which states that matter is the only reality, and that mind, feelings and so on, are only functions of matter. It is also opposed to realism, the view that we see things as they really are, independent of the mind.

George Berkeley (1685–1753), an Irish bishop, is generally regarded as the first idealist philosopher. His 'subjective idealism' holds that material objects only exist in so far as they are perceived by the mind, a doctrine encapsulated in the dictum *Esse est percipi* ('To be is to be perceived'). Only things that are perceived are real, and the things perceived are ideas that only exist in the mind.

The 'transcendental idealism' of the German philosopher Immanuel Kant (1724–1804) distinguishes between appearances and reality. Appearances, Kant says, are only representations, not 'things-in-themselves'. He goes on to assert that time and space are human mental constructs, 'not determinations given as existing by themselves, nor conditions of objects viewed as things-in-themselves'.

A third strand is 'absolute idealism', as developed by the German philosopher G.W.F. Hegel (1770–1831). In this, the distinction between consciousness and its object breaks down, giving rise to the notion of the Absolute, some sort of universal mind, in which the real is perfect, whole and complete. Such bold metaphysical claims have inspired much scepticism. Nevertheless, the idealistic tendency endures in the philosophical approach known as phenomenology (see page 82).

Materialism

In philosophy, materialism is the doctrine that nothing exists apart from matter. Mind itself can be explained in purely material terms, as can history – for example, Karl Marx (opppsite) proposed a theory of dialectical materialism, which portrays historical developments as the result of blind economic forces (see page 260). Materialism is thus the opposite of idealism (see page 62).

The earliest materialist account of reality is that of the Greek philosopher Democritus (*c.*460–*c.*370 BC), who suggested that the world is made up of tiny indivisible particles he called atoms – one of the first scientific theories. As science has advanced, and it has been discovered that the physical world is made up of fields and forces, for example, as well as matter, materialist philosophers have had to adjust their definition of reality to encompass all that can be studied by the scientific method (see page 162). This is close to positivism (see page 66).

Positivism

Positivism is a movement that originated with the French philosopher Auguste Comte (1798–1857), who coined the term. Comte believed that human society has evolved through three stages of intellectual development: the religious, the metaphysical and the scientific or 'positive'. He suggested a hierarchy of the sciences, resting on the base of mathematics, upon which was built physics, then chemistry, then biology, then sociology – which he named, and which he sought to establish as a scientific discipline.

Positivism rejects theology and metaphysics on the grounds that they involve speculation beyond the scope of experience. It thus dismisses pursuits of first causes (see page 48) or purposes (see page 30) as fruitless. Positivists state that true knowledge is restricted to what can be derived from sense data, specifically scientific experiment and observation. Positivism is thus related to both materialism (see page 64) and empiricism (see page 70).

During the 19th century, as science began to take a central role in Western intellectual life, positivists turned to a critical examination of the assumptions and methods of science. Positivists were suspicious of scientific theories and concepts, as compared to experiments and observations. They distrusted the claims of scientific theories to absolute truth and suggested that they were only useful in so far as they could make predictions (a position similar to pragmatism; see page 78). Explanation itself was seen as no more than a way of organizing experimental data and observations.

As a consequence of their insistence on observability, positivists fell into the trap of dismissing the concept of the atom as a 'convenient fiction'. They were similarly sceptical of causality (see page 72), preferring to think of a regularity in the succession of observed events.

In the 20th century, positivists began to focus more on logic and language, giving rise to logical positivism (see page 80) and converging with analytic or linguistic philosophy (see page 94).

Rationalism

In the philosophical context, the term 'rationalism' denotes the approach and methods advocated by the French philosopher René Descartes (1596–1650). Descartes began by asking 'How and what do I know?' His method was to doubt everything, including the evidence of an external world supplied by his senses. There was no irrefutable, rational reason why he should accept this evidence as true, he argued. The only certainty he was left with was that he knew he was thinking: *Cogito ergo sum,* 'I think therefore I am.'

From this certainty, he sought to demonstrate – by rational deduction from first principles – the existence of everything, including God. In the process he created a dualism between two entirely different substances, mind and matter, which somehow interact (see page 43). Descartes' method of arguing from general principles to particular conclusions without regard to observations of the physical world was challenged by the empiricists (see page 70).

Descartes believed the workings of the human body could be deduced from mathematical and geometrical principles.

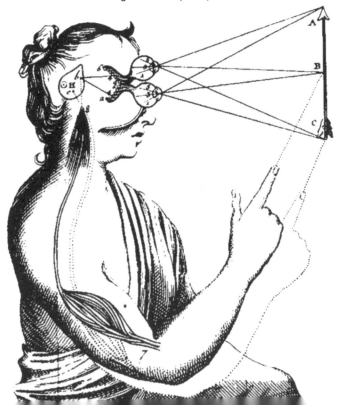

Empiricism

Empiricism is the philosophical doctrine that holds that all knowledge ultimately derives from experience (Greek *empeiria*) – in other words, from the evidence of the external world supplied to us by our senses. There are no such things as innate ideas or *a priori* concepts – concepts that are independent of experience, but which are held to derive from the nature or structure of the mind. Only *a posteriori* concepts – those derived from experience – have any validity. Empiricism is thus opposed to rationalism (see page 68).

The English philosopher and statesman Francis Bacon (1561–1626) was one of the first advocates of empirical methods in science. He championed induction – the derivation of general theories from what is seen to happen in the physical world. This approach was triumphantly vindicated by Sir Isaac Newton, who used mathematics to derive the laws of motion and gravitation from his observations (see page 178).

Following in the tradition of Bacon, John Locke (1632–1704), another Englishman, is generally regarded as the first empiricist philosopher. In *An Essay Concerning Human Understanding* (1690) he dismissed the rationalism of Descartes, arguing that there are no such things as innate ideas. At birth, he maintained, the mind is a *tabula rasa* or blank slate, and the only knowledge we have is acquired via the senses from experience.

In the following century, the Scottish philosopher David Hume (1711–76) re-examined the way that people behave and think, rejecting rationalism in favour of a sceptical psychological approach. Hume concluded that humans are governed by desire more than reason, and that ideas derive from impressions, via such processes as memory and imagination. The way we think is determined by 'custom': our moral judgements are based on feelings rather than abstract moral principles, and such notions as causality (see page 72), he asserted, are merely mental habits.

Causality

Much of our picture of the world is based on causality — the idea of cause leading inexorably to effect. For determinists (see page 46), everything that ever was, is or will be is linked in this way. Causes can be distinguished from reasons. If I give a reason for an action, I am describing a motive. If I give a reason for a belief, I am presenting a justification.

Science is largely based on the linking of causes and effects, although the sceptical Scottish philosopher David Hume argued that there is logically no absolute certainty in deriving a general principle from repeated observations of one thing (such as pricking one's finger) leading to another (such as feeling pain). All we can talk about is a 'constant conjunction'. With the advent of quantum physics and the principle of indeterminacy (see page 183), science itself has had to recognize the limits of causality.

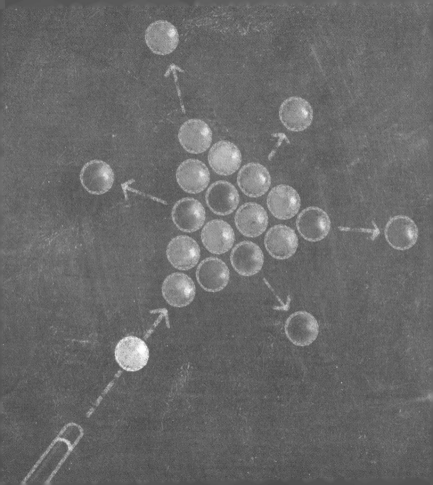

Scepticism

Scepticism (from the Greek *skeptikos*, 'an inquirer') is a philosophical approach that casts doubt on assumptions and proclaimed certainties. Moderate sceptics question particular knowledge claims in furtherance of establishing the truth. Extreme sceptics hold that absolute knowledge of anything is unachievable.

Scepticism is at the heart of the Western philosophical tradition. In the 5th century BC, Parmenides and others cast doubt on the reality of change and motion (see page 44), while Socrates constantly challenged the knowledge claims of others. Pyrrho (*c*.360–*c*.270 BC) went even further, asserting that tranquillity could only be achieved by rejecting all claims to certainty. Other ancient sceptics questioned whether any criteria could ever be established for distinguishing between what is true and what is not, although some concluded that decisions could be based on balances of probabilities.

Scepticism played little role in Christian thought in the Middle Ages, but with the Reformation and the Scientific Revolution, the certainties proclaimed by the Roman Catholic Church began to be questioned. In the 17th century, René Descartes used the methods of scepticism to re-establish certainty (see page 68), but his doubts regarding the reliability of what our senses tell us were challenged as unreasonable and contrary to common sense by empiricists such as John Locke (see page 70).

In the 18th century, David Hume, though an empiricist, took extreme sceptical positions in relation to a number of concepts, such as causality (see page 72). Even reason was not immune: Hume asserted that neither induction nor deduction (see pages 86–7) are capable of establishing the truth of any matter of fact. Our beliefs about the world derive not from reason or evidence, he argued, but from custom and habit. Although it is natural for us to believe in a self and an external world, even a God, Hume denied that there was sufficient evidence to justify such beliefs. Appeals to 'common sense' (see page 76) simply sidestep the issues.

Common sense

Many of the more challenging positions that have been arrived at by philosophers have been criticized on the grounds that they run counter to 'common sense'. 'Common sense' tells us we perceive the external world directly, and that what we see is how things are. Thus 'common sense' is used, for example, to refute Plato's suggestion that ultimate reality cannot be grasped via the senses (see page 14).

The extreme scepticism of David Hume (see page 75) as regards the existence of the external world and the human soul was denounced by a fellow Scot, Thomas Reid (1710–96), founder of the 'Common Sense' school, on the grounds that their existence is self-evident 'by the consent of ages and nations, of the learned and the unlearned'. This hardly constitutes evidence, but merely accords authority to tradition and unthinking prejudice. Appearances can be deceptive. After all, common sense would tell us that the world is flat, and that the Sun revolves around the Earth, not the other way round.

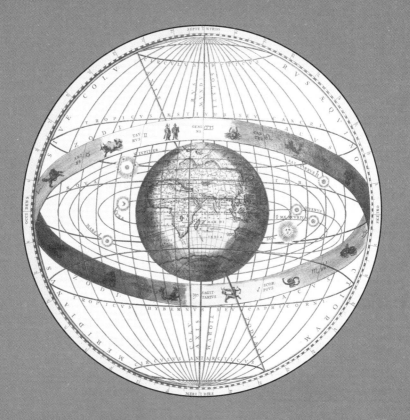

Pragmatism and instrumentalism

Pragmatism is a philosophical movement that arose in the USA in the late 19th century. In the words of American psychologist and philosopher William James (1842–1910), the pragmatist 'turns away from abstraction and insufficiency, from verbal solutions, from bad *a priori* reasons, from fixed principles, closed systems, and pretended absolutes. He turns towards concreteness and adequacy, towards facts, towards action.'

Pragmatism was initiated by James's friend, the US philosopher C.S. Peirce (1839–1914), who first enunciated what became known as the 'pragmatic maxim' in 1878: 'Consider what effects, that might conceivably have practical bearings, we conceive the object of our conception to have. Then, our conception of these effects is the whole of our conception of the object.' In other words, the truth of a proposition can only be judged by its practical outcomes. Thus the metaphysical speculations of the continental European tradition were dismissed as meaningless, as their truth or falsity had no practical impact on human affairs.

The US philosopher and educationalist John Dewey (1859–1952) developed a form of pragmatism known as instrumentalism. This asserts that the value of any scientific theory lies not in its truth, but in its usefulness, for example in making predictions. Dewey held that there was no reality other than that encountered through everyday experience and scientific inquiry. Education, he advocated, should be directed towards problem-solving.

William James extended the pragmatic approach to ethical principles and religious beliefs, holding that such principles or beliefs are 'true' in so far as they prove useful, for example by increasing a person's well-being. However, various philosophers have been critical of James's identification of true beliefs with useful ones, asserting that some beliefs can be both useful and demonstrably false. Other philosophers have dismissed pragmatism as a typically American success-oriented approach, which simply ignores a range of difficult philosophical questions.

Logical positivism

Logical positivism was a philosophical movement that originated in Vienna in the 1920s. It insists that only scientific knowledge is factual, and that the role of philosophy is to clarify basic concepts and assertions. Thus all the questions raised in metaphysics, ethics and aesthetics – such as, 'What is being?' or 'What is good?' – are dismissed as meaningless. Any answers supplied cannot be shown to be either true or false.

Logical positivism states that a proposition must be verifiable to have meaning. There are two ways in which a proposition can be verified. Firstly, it can be empirically tested. The statement 'This stone has a mass of 10 kilos' can be verified by weighing the stone. Secondly, a proposition such as 'The sparrow is a species of bird' can be tested against the definition of the words used, and the grammatical structure. Later philosophers found logical positivism too restrictive, and developed more subtle theories of language and meaning.

Logical positivism tests statements such as 'The sparrow is a species of bird' against their grammar and definitions. For instance: 'What is a sparrow?', 'What is a bird?' and 'What is a species?'

Phenomenology

Phenomenology is a philosophical approach that investigates phenomena as objects of perception, rather than independently existing facts or events. Theories about existence and causation are eschewed in favour of examinations of the way humans think about and interpret the world.

Phenomenology was founded in the early 20th century by the German philosopher Edmund Husserl (1859–1938). Husserl sought to examine the structures of consciousness, and the phenomena that occur within consciousness, and believed that this approach could establish a firm foundation for all human knowledge, including scientific knowledge.

Phenomenology subsequently became an important strand in 20th-century philosophy, especially in Germany and France, and Husserl's ideas were further developed and criticized by various other philosophers and sociologists, including existentialists such as Martin Heidegger and Jean-Paul Sartre (see page 37).

Phenomenology can be seen as a type of idealism (see page 62). Phenomenologists hold that there are two types of knowledge, direct and indirect. We know essences, i.e. universal properties such as 'blueness' or 'sphericity', directly. Such essences we can grasp in their entirety through a single mental act. But we only know objects of perception (for example, a blue ball) indirectly, through their 'aspects'. For example, we can only see one half of the ball at a time, and if the light comes from the side, for example, there will be a shadow cast that makes the ball appear to be made up of different shades of blue. This form of understanding is indirect knowledge.

In contrast, mental acts, such as the act of seeing a blue ball, or the memory of a delicious meal, are known to us in their entirety, without aspects. Thus consciousness, and the objects of the world of consciousness, are – like essences but unlike the objects of perception – known directly. Phenomenologists therefore emphasize the importance of studying the essences of our mental acts, eschewing the empiricism of science.

The other minds problem

One of the questions that continues to trouble philosophers (and inquisitive children of a certain age) is this: How can I tell that anybody else has a mind? I know that I am conscious, have thoughts and feelings, perceive the colour red as red, find the sensation of burning painful, and so on. But how can I tell whether anybody else does? All I can observe is the outward behaviour of others. So how do I know they are not just zombies?

Of course, common sense tells us this is a fuss about nothing, but it is nevertheless true that there is no way of conclusively proving the existence of other minds. The best we can do is to argue from analogy. We observe so many instances of other people responding to stimuli as we do, that it seems justifiable to believe that, just as their physiology and behaviour resembles ours, their minds must do so as well.

Logic and argument

Logic is that branch of philosophy that focuses on whether arguments are good or bad, i.e. whether they are valid. It is concerned not with the content of an argument, but on its formal properties and structure.

To be valid, an argument has to demonstrate or prove a point (a conclusion) from accepted foundations (premises) in such a way that to accept the premises but deny the conclusion would be inconsistent. The premises themselves may be established by empirical observation, from the conclusions of previous arguments, or by definition. However, they must not depend on the conclusion, otherwise the argument will be circular.

The argument 'All animals with wings can fly; pigs have wings; therefore pigs can fly' might seem utter nonsense. And yet formally it is a valid argument, even though we know that neither of the two premises nor the conclusion are true. The point is, if we accept both premises, we would contradict ourselves if we denied the truth of the conclusion. The kind of reasoning used in this argument is known as deduction, which derives particular truths from general principles.

The other main type of argument is induction, which derives general principles from particular observed facts. An example of this kind of argument is 'No one has ever seen a swan that was not white; therefore all swans are white.' For centuries this might have seemed a reasonable argument, but of course when European settlers first explored Australia, they did indeed discover black swans.

Inductive arguments can never be valid in the same way as deductive arguments. The conclusion is never implicit in the premises; the premises can only supply evidence in support of the probability of the conclusion being true. And yet, of course, most of the decisions and actions we take in the real world are based on induction – as is most of science (see page 162).

The traditional logic outlined above is known as 'formal logic'. Since the early 20th century, developments have mostly been in the field of 'symbolic' logic, which is close to mathematics.

Syllogisms

Traditional logic, known as 'formal logic', is based on the three-part argument known as the syllogism, which comprises three propositions: two premises and a conclusion derived from the two premises. For example, 'All Greeks are human; all humans are mortal; therefore all Greeks are mortal.'

The propositions may take any of the following forms: 'All X are Y', 'No X are Y', 'Some X are Y' and 'Some X are not Y'. A syllogism has three terms: one of them, the 'middle term' (swans) appears in both premises; the second (white) appears in the conclusion and one of the premises; the third (birds) appears in the conclusion and the other premise.

The first term (the 'subject') of the conclusion is known as the 'minor term', and the premise in which it appears is the 'minor premise'. The second term (the 'predicate') of the conclusion is the 'major term', and the premise in which it appears is the 'major premise'.

Some swans are white.
Some birds are swans.
Therefore some birds are white.

Category errors

Various philosophers have attempted to draw up lists of fundamental categories to which things or concepts can be ascribed. Such categories are intended to be irreducible to anything simpler.

Aristotle, for example, came up with a list of ten, including substance, quantity, quality and relation. The German philosopher Immanuel Kant (see page 63) offered a dozen, including time, space, things, properties, one and many, as the basic constructs through which the mind comprehends reality.

Although no list of fundamental categories has been universally accepted by philosophers, they are generally in agreement that it is a mistake to present something belonging to one category as if it belonged to another, or to ascribe to something in one category a property that can only belong to another category. For example, it makes no sense to ascribe smells to music, or emotions to stones – unless, of course, one is speaking metaphorically. Poetry, after all, is full of figurative language that does not make literal sense, but nevertheless has meaning. We all know what Wordsworth means when he writes 'My heart leaps up when I behold a rainbow in the sky', even though we know his heart stays in exactly the same position within his chest.

Poetry aside, many apparent problems and difficulties in intellectual debate can be blamed on category errors. The term itself was introduced by the English philosopher Gilbert Ryle in *The Concept of Mind* (1949). Here, Ryle gives the example of the visitor to Oxford, who is shown the colleges, libraries and so on, and then asks 'But where is the university?'

Ryle goes on to criticize the dualism of René Descartes (see page 43) – in which body and mind are seen as different substances, one material, one immaterial – as a category error. It is a mistake, Ryle contends, to apply the 'substance' label to the mind, which he asserts is no more than the intelligent behaviour of the body.

Paradoxes

The paradoxes devised by philosophers are apparently self-contradictory statements that are intended to show up some inadequacy in our use of language or in our ways of thinking. Examples discussed elsewhere include the Achilles paradox (see page 45) and the liar paradox (see page 57).

One of the most challenging paradoxes is the heap paradox, dating back (like those mentioned above) to ancient Greece. This points out that one grain of sand does not make a heap,

and if one grain does not, then neither do two, three or four. So at what point does adding a single grain of sand to our collection of grains make a heap?

The heap paradox has many implications, for example in the debate about abortion: at what point does the foetus, initially a collection of just a few cells, become a living person? This type of paradox teaches us about the nature of continuums, where there is no single definable point at which one thing becomes another.

A variant of the heap paradox: at what point does the loss of a little more hair make the man bald?

Language and meaning

One of the most important strands in modern philosophy is the philosophy of language. A great deal of effort has been expended to elucidate the nature of language, and how we actually use it. As a result, many of the theories that philosophers came up with in the past have been shown to arise from misunderstandings of how language works.

Traditionally, philosophers have assumed that the meaning of a word is simply its 'reference', the thing it stands for. This works well in many cases, but becomes problematic when we are dealing with things that do not exist. Just because we have the word 'ghost', it does not necessarily follow that such an entity is real. It was this trap that led Plato into believing that general terms such as 'horse', 'circle' or 'good' actually existed as abstract, immaterial Forms (see page 14).

At the end of the 19th century, German philosopher Gottlob Frege (1848–1925) suggested that a word has a 'sense' as well as a reference. Different words can have the same reference, but different senses: for example, the names Elton John and Reginald Dwight refer to the same person, but the first is a celebrity and the latter is a private individual.

Subsequently, the logical positivists insisted that only statements that could be verified – either by empirical testing or by virtue of the definitions of the words used, and the grammatical structure – had any meaning at all (see page 80).

The highly influential Austrian philosopher Ludwig Wittgenstein (1889–1951) developed a very different approach, suggesting that the meaning of a word or expression depends on its use – in other words, upon social conventions. Humans play different 'language games' in different contexts: for example, a statement that has meaning within a poem might well be nonsensical in the context of a scientific paper. Wittgenstein's approach to language and meaning has proved enormously influential in the field of philosophy.

Language and thought

To what extent is thinking dependent upon language? Can we actually think at all without language? The questions depend upon what we mean both by 'thinking' and by 'language'. Planning the future would seem to fit the description 'thinking', and planning what I am going to cook for dinner tonight might consist entirely of visual images – especially if I can't remember the names for certain exotic ingredients, of which I nevertheless have a clear conception.

Deductive reasoning would appear to require language, assuming that mathematics or symbolic logic count as 'languages'. And if they do, how about music? Composers draw on the 'language' of melody, harmony and rhythm to create pieces, and if we run a tune through our heads we are using that language. In contrast, however, learning is a form of thought that often involves deriving general principles from particular experiences (induction), and infants and laboratory rats, for example, seem able to achieve this without language.

Ethics

Ethics – also known as moral philosophy – seeks to examine the meaning of moral terms and the criteria by which we make moral judgements. It is not to be confused with moral teaching – the laying down of what is right and wrong (see page 100). In practice, however, philosophers have not always made a sharp distinction between the two, and in many fields – such as human rights, punishment, medicine and so on – debates on ethical issues are used as guides to practical decision-making.

Among the ancient Greeks, both Plato and Aristotle sought to define what constitutes the 'good life'. Both associated it with happiness, which in turn comes from living in accordance with virtues such as temperance, courage, piety and justice. Reason for them is the best guide to behaviour. Plato believed that 'the good' was an abstract Form (see page 14) beyond the everyday world, while Aristotle saw virtue as natural to human beings.

In the European Middle Ages, St Thomas Aquinas sought to integrate Aristotelian ethics with Christian theology (see page 136). He argued that God had designed humans to follow the 'natural law' of their natures, and that this natural law coincides with the divine law.

This raises a question first broached by Plato: Is the good good solely because God commands it, or does God command it because it is good? If the former, in what sense is it moral to pursue it; if the latter, why bring in God at all?

In the modern period, one of the most significant debates has concerned ends and means. Deontology holds that the rightness of an action should be judged in so far as it conforms to one's duty, irrespective of the consequences. In the 18th century Immanuel Kant described injunctions such as 'Do not lie' or 'Do not kill' as 'categorical imperatives' – principles that must be obeyed absolutely and unconditionally in all circumstances (see page 119). In contrast, consequentialist theories, such as utilitarianism (see page 116), judge actions solely or largely by their outcomes.

Morality

The term 'morality' denotes a system of beliefs as to what is good and bad. It also denotes conformity to conventional standards of moral conduct. Deliberate flouting of those standards is termed 'immorality', while those who do not adhere to such standards out of ignorance, or because they have no sense of right or wrong, are termed 'amoral'.

Morality assumes a community of people who hold each other responsible for their actions, and a shared set of values. In many cultures, moral principles are regarded as divinely ordained, and thus morality consists of obedience to authority. Law is generally regarded as the means of implementing morality, although there is not always a consensus as to which laws are just. Views as to what is moral vary from society to society (see relativism, page 334), although some assert that there are, for example, universal human rights that transcend cultural differences (see page 292).

Hogarth's *Industry and Idleness* warns of the consequences of immorality.

Good

The way we use language often lures us into misapprehensions. A case in point is the word 'good', which we use in a variety of ways. Most commonly, it is used as an adjective. We speak of a 'good person' or a 'good deed', a 'good film', a 'good car', and so on. On the surface of it, this would suggest that there is some quality, 'goodness', that is possessed by all the things that we designate 'good'.

But it is clear that these things have no significant *intrinsic* property in common. In saying a person or an action is good we are making a moral judgement; in saying a film is good we are making an aesthetic judgement; and in saying a car is good we are commending such things as its functionality, comfort or economy.

However, these things may have an *extrinsic* property in common, in that they all, in some way or another, satisfy some human interest. Some philosophers deny that the use of the word 'good' implies any kind of property, but merely expresses our approval.

In philosophical discourse, 'good' is also used as a noun, and philosophers often distinguish between 'intrinsic goods', or 'goods-in-themselves', and 'extrinsic goods'. Aristotle gave health as an example of an intrinsic good, something that is pursued for its own sake, and cited money as an example of an extrinsic good, i.e. one that is pursued for its consequences.

Some philosophers and theologians have talked of 'the greatest good'. Plato conceived of the good as the highest of the abstract, immaterial Forms (see page 14), while Aristotle saw the highest good for humans as the exercise of the virtues, by means of which they can achieve the good life, or well-being.

Other thinkers variously conceive of the greatest good in terms of the fulfilment of God's purpose, for example, or love, or happiness, or pleasure, or living in harmony with others and with nature.

Evil

Moral evil comprises the pain and suffering that results when humans act in a way that is morally wrong. In contrast, 'natural evil' results from such things as disease or natural disasters. In theology, evil has been regarded as an abstract but real entity, personified by the Devil; it is the origin and inspiration of evil things, people and actions. Since the Fall, it is human nature to be sinful (see pages 20 and 146). The question as to why an omnipotent and benevolent God allows evil to exist has long troubled theologians (see page 152).

Moral philosophers are more concerned with questions regarding what can be regarded as evil. For example, are certain actions (such as killing) always wrong, regardless of the good that comes out of them (such as defeating Nazism)? In other words, do ends ever justify means? Similarly, if someone intends to do good, and in so doing unintentionally commits an evil act, are they themselves evil?

William Blake depicts Satan inflicting extreme suffering on Job to test the limits of his faith.

The golden mean

The phrase 'golden mean' denotes the middle course between two extremes, and suggests balance and harmony. The concept is found in a number of philosophies of the good life. In Buddhism, for example, the golden mean is the 'middle way' between sensual luxury and self-mortification, while according to Confucian tradition, 'The virtue embodied in the doctrine of the mean is of the highest order. But it has long been rare among people.'

In ancient Greece, Socrates applied the idea to education, suggesting that exclusive devotion to gymnastics breeds hardness and ferocity, while those who devote themselves solely to music become soft and effeminate. Combining the two pursuits results in harmony, in the form of beauty and goodness. In Plato's dialogue *Philebus*, Socrates states that 'measure and proportion manifest themselves in all areas of beauty and virtue'.

In the ethics of Aristotle, the golden mean similarly provides the guide to virtue and right action. He describes it thus: 'Virtue, then, is a state of character concerned with choice, lying in the mean which is defined by reference to reason. It is a mean between two vices, one of excess and one of deficiency; and again, it is a mean because the vices respectively fall short or exceed what is right in both passions and actions, while virtue both finds and chooses that which is intermediate.'

For Aristotle, virtue lies between two extremes, and must be guided by reason. For example, the virtue of courage lies between the extremes of recklessness (an excess of courage) and cowardice (a deficiency of courage). The ideal of the golden mean demands that the virtuous person responds to the right degree to promptings to action, on the right occasions, for the right reasons, and in relation to the right people.

Happiness

Some philosophers have claimed that happiness is the greatest good. But what do they mean by 'happiness'? The doctrine known as hedonism, originating in ancient Greece, largely associates happiness with pleasure (see page 110). In contrast, Aristotle and others associate happiness with leading the good life, which consists of using reason both in thought and as a guide to virtuous action.

Both interpretations of happiness are found in the aim of utilitarianism, which is to achieve 'the greatest happiness of the greatest number' (see page 116). This is a goal that many politicians lay claim to, and in the American Declaration of Independence, 'the pursuit of happiness' is numbered as a fundamental human right. However, some have suggested that the pursuit of happiness is itself a source of unhappiness. Others associate happiness with contentment, and contentment with servility: a pig may be happy in its muck, but it is not free.

Hedonism

Hedonism is an ethical theory originating in ancient Greece, which holds that happiness is the greatest good, and should therefore be the main goal of life. Happiness is largely associated with pleasure (Greek *hedone*), although the nature of pleasure itself is variously defined. Hedonism is not always a matter of merely indulging oneself in sensual pleasures. As the American philosopher and psychologist William James (see page 78) observed, 'If merely "feeling good" could decide, drunkenness would be the supremely valid human experience.'

For the philosophers of the Cyrenaic school, founded around 400 BC by Aristippus of Cyrene, the supreme good was the pleasure of the moment, associated with 'smooth motion of the flesh'. Aristippus pointed out that all animals seek to pursue pleasure and avoid pain, and was sceptical that anything could be known beyond immediate physical sensations.

However, pleasure for Aristippus was not just a matter of abandoned self-indulgence: he emphasized that reason and self-control were essential in choosing the best pleasures. When criticized for consorting with a courtesan he retorted, 'I possess her, but am not possessed by her; for to control pleasures without being mastered by them is better than not to control them at all.'

Another Greek school, the Epicureans, founded by Epicurus (341–270 BC), also saw pleasure as the greatest good. Pleasure, Epicurus argued, was to be achieved by avoiding pain, both mental and physical, and this could best be achieved by reducing desire and focusing on mental rather than physical pleasures. Thus the greatest pleasure is found in a serene detachment. 'It is impossible to live a pleasant life without living wisely and well and justly,' he declared, 'and it is impossible to live wisely and well and justly without living pleasantly.'

More recently, hedonism has resurfaced in the form of utilitarianism, the doctrine that individual action and social policy should be directed towards producing 'the greatest happiness of the greatest number' (see page 116).

Cynicism

Today, a 'cynic' is someone who thinks the worst of people, and who is convinced that everything will turn out badly. The word is also applied to someone who disregards moral principles in pursuit of their aims. The word derives from the Greek *kunikos*, 'dog-like', and in ancient Greece the disparaging term 'Cynics' was applied to a philosophical sect founded by Antisthenes (c.444–c. 366 BC), a follower of Socrates.

The Cynics were compared to dogs by their contemporaries largely on account of their rejection of conventional social values. In their place, they advocated a strict asceticism, believing that virtue is to be found living a life in harmony with nature, and rejecting pleasure, comfort and wealth. Diogenes (c.412–c.323 BC), one of the most famous Cynics, took his nickname 'the Dog' seriously, wandering the streets naked, defecating in public, sleeping in a tub or barrel in the local marketplace and barking at those he regarded as having departed from the path of virtue.

Stoicism

Stoicism is a philosophical tradition founded in ancient Greece around 300 BC by Zeno of Citium. It took its name from the Stoa Poikile ('painted porch'), part of the agora or assembly place in Athens where Zeno taught. The influence of the Stoics extends down to the present day – we still use the word 'stoical' to denote an attitude in which misfortune is endured without complaint.

Influenced by the Cynics (see page 112), another primarily ethical school, the Stoics placed great emphasis on wisdom and virtue, which were strongly identified with each other. Their ethics derived from their metaphysics. The Stoics were pantheists and materialists: for them, God was identified with reason, which was regarded as the underlying principle of the universe, and humans themselves partook of the divine fire. The wise man lived in harmony with nature, and accepted both good and ill fortune with equanimity.

At times, the ethics of the Stoics can seem heartless and almost inhumanely stern to our modern sensibility. For example, the wise man of the Stoics would, if he saw his child drowning, attempt to save it. But if he failed, and the child died, he would feel no regret or sorrow. Knowing he had done his best, he would recognize that the child's death must have been part of a divine plan, and so be for the best.

The early Stoics believed that all men are brothers, and condemned slavery. From around the 1st century BC, Stoicism was adopted by the elite of Roman society, and more stress was placed on the importance of duty. Notable Roman Stoics include the playwright Seneca (*c*.4 BC–AD 65) and the Emperor Marcus Aurelius (AD 121–180), whose *Meditations* include such aphorisms as 'Men exist for the sake of one another; either teach them or bear with them' and 'Let thy every action, word and thought be that of one who is prepared at any moment to quit this life.'

Utilitarianism

Utilitarianism is a system of practical ethics devised by the English philosopher and reformer Jeremy Bentham (1748–1832), who famously stated that 'The greatest happiness of the greatest number is the foundation of morals and legislation.' Utilitarianism is thus a form of hedonism (see page 110). Bentham (opposite) developed a simple 'moral calculus', asserting that the pleasure and pain produced by an action could be quantified, and the action thereby judged good or evil.

For English philosopher John Stuart Mill (1806–73), Bentham's version of utilitarianism was too crude. Mill emphasized the importance of the quality of pleasures, placing greatest value on 'the pleasures of the intellect, of the feelings and imagination, and of the moral sentiments'. Mill also modified the inflexible Benthamite calculus by standing up for the rights of the individual against the majority. Although criticized by some as an example of the naturalistic fallacy (see page 123), utilitarianism continues to have great influence on social policy.

The Golden Rule

The 'Golden Rule' is encapsulated in the proverb 'Do as ye would be done by.' It was famously enunciated by Jesus in Luke 6:31: 'And as ye would that men should do to you, do ye also to them likewise.' This 'Golden Rule' is also a cornerstone for ethical behaviour in many other religious and moral traditions. For example, several centuries before Jesus, Confucius gave the following negative version as the guiding principle for conduct throughout life: 'Do not do to others what you do not want them to do to you.'

Our ability to put ourselves in another's shoes – the human quality known as empathy – and to act accordingly, is fundamental to social relationships. Without the Golden Rule, it would not be possible to have a such a thing as a society; and the Golden Rule, with its inherent principles of justice and fairness for all, lies at the root of most systems of law.

Some have sought to mock the Golden Rule by proffering facetious counter-examples. Would we wish for the masochist to deal out treatment to others that he himself would welcome? But this misses the point: the Golden Rule does not endorse particular moral principles, nor does it provide the basis for moral choice independent of other principles of conduct. It merely demands consistency.

The 18th-century German philosopher Immanuel Kant asserted that the Golden Rule had insufficient rigour to be counted as a universal law. In its place he formulated the 'categorical imperative', which he stated thus: 'Act only in accordance with a maxim that you can at the same time will to become a universal law.' Thus, if I tell a lie to further my own interests, or dodge my bus fare, for example, I must ask myself what the consequences would be if everybody behaved like me. Only thus can I avoid narrow self-interest and moral myopia.

Acts and omissions

Moral philosophers and theologians have long pondered the relative moral status of an act as opposed to an omission, where both have the same outcome. For example, is there a moral difference between telling a lie and remaining silent, and thus failing to tell the truth? Or between killing and allowing to die?

The question highlights the major fault line in ethical thinking between consequentialists and deontologists – between those who believe that ends justify means and those who do not. Consequentialists judge acts and omissions only (or predominantly) on their outcomes. In contrast, deontologists are concerned with doing one's duty: but here the question arises whether, for example, the duty not to kill is a more fundamental moral imperative than the duty to save lives. In general, the law asserts that deliberate killing is murder, while negligence that leads to death attracts the lesser charge of manslaughter.

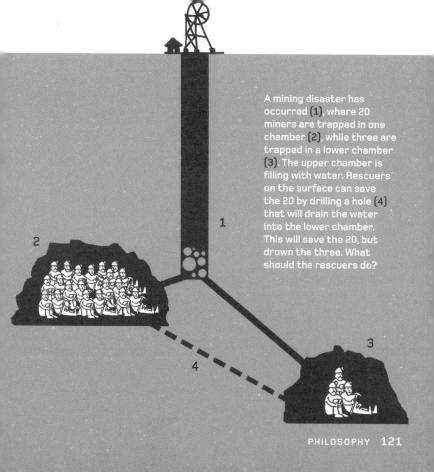

A mining disaster has occurred (1), where 20 miners are trapped in one chamber (2), while three are trapped in a lower chamber (3). The upper chamber is filling with water. Rescuers on the surface can save the 20 by drilling a hole (4) that will drain the water into the lower chamber. This will save the 20, but drown the three. What should the rescuers do?

The is/ought problem

'In every system of morality, which I have hitherto met with,' wrote the Scottish philosopher David Hume in *A Treatise on Human Nature* (1736), 'I have always remarked, that the author proceeds for some time in the ordinary way of reasoning, and establishes the being of a god, or makes observations concerning human affairs; when of a sudden I am surprised to find that instead of the usual copulations of proposition, is and is not, I meet with no proposition that is not connected with an ought or an ought not. This change is imperceptible; but it is, however, of the last consequence.'

What Hume was highlighting was the human tendency to equate moral statements with objective facts – to suggest that 'Killing is wrong' has the same force of truth as, for example, 'The Earth orbits the Sun'. Hume denied that it is ever possible to deduce value judgements from factual premises, arguing that we base our moral judgements not on reason, but on sentiment.

In the early 20th century the English moral philosopher G.E. Moore (1873–1958) gave a name to the derivation of moral conclusions from factual premises: he called it the 'naturalistic fallacy'. Moore, in an implicit criticism of utilitarianism (see page 116), asserted that it was not possible to define 'good' in terms of descriptive expressions such as 'happiness' or 'pleasure'. Goodness, Moore claimed, cannot be identified via empirical observation, but only via some autonomous moral faculty – a position known as intuitionism.

An awareness of the dangers of the naturalistic fallacy – of deriving an 'ought' from an 'is' – is important in the scrutiny of a wide range of issues. For example, Darwin's theory of evolution by natural selection suggests that new, better-adapted species evolve via 'the survival of the fittest' (see page 196). However, just because this is the case in nature, ought we to adopt the principle – as social Darwinists do (see page 242) – as the way for humans to behave in a civilized society?

Emotivism and prescriptivism

The naturalistic fallacy – of deriving an 'ought' from an 'is' – gave rise in the 20th century to the theory known as emotivism, also known as the 'boo-hurrah theory'. Developed in the 1930s by the English philosopher A.J. Ayer (1910–89), emotivism holds that moral statements, although grammatically resembling statements of fact, do no more than express the feelings of the speaker, whether of approval or disapproval. If we say, 'Killing is wrong', what we are actually saying is, 'Boo to murder!' If we say, 'Not lying is good', we are actually saying, 'Hurrah for telling the truth!'

A further development of emotivism is prescriptivism, which was advocated by another English philosopher, R.M. Hare (1919–2002). Prescriptivism holds that moral statements are like imperatives. They not only express the attitude of the speaker, but also commit the speaker, and guide others, to a certain course of action. In contrast, accepting a statement of fact only commits the speaker to a belief.

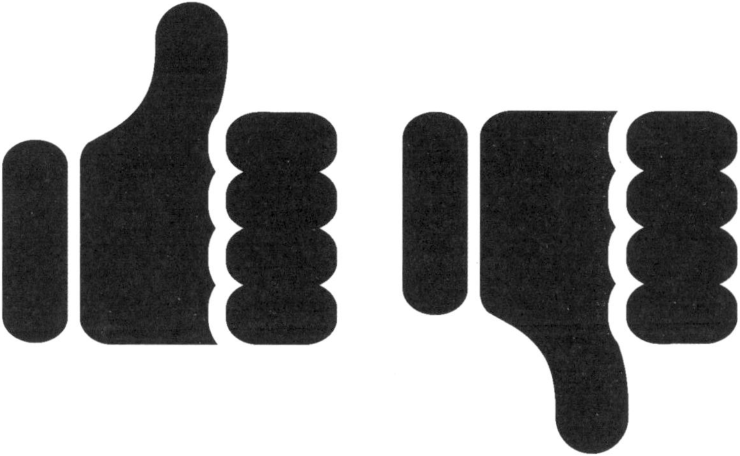

Aesthetics

Aesthetics is the branch of philosophy that examines the nature of beauty, and the grounds upon which we make critical judgements about works of art. It may also ask questions such as 'What is art?' and 'What, if anything, is art for?'

One of the most enduring conceptions of art is that it is representational – it imitates the world we observe, holding, in Hamlet's words, 'the mirror up to nature' (see Mimesis, page 374). In ancient Greece, Plato held that ideal beauty – like ideal goodness – only exists as one of the immaterial Forms (see page 14). Actual works of art are therefore no more than inferior imitations, and not to be trusted as guides to either truth or goodness. For this reason, Plato banned poets and other artists from his ideal Republic.

In contrast, Aristotle believed that works of art improve upon nature, and provide an insight into the universal essence of things. He held that art has a positive social value: tragedy, for example, by eliciting feelings of 'pity and terror' in the audience, has the useful role of purging our emotions.

As far as judging the quality of a work of art, Aristotle laid out certain criteria. Tragedy, for instance, has to possess 'unity of action' (to which later commentators added unities of time and place). For Plato, the excellence of a piece of music, for example, is to be judged by the extent to which it delights those who are 'pre-eminent in virtue and education'.

The idea that only an educated elite are equipped to judge the quality of a work of art continues to this day. However, the criteria by which critics judge works of art have shifted over the centuries. In the visual arts, for example, the value of sheer representational brilliance was eclipsed by the invention of photography. 'Expressive' qualities became more important (see page 398), as did 'formal' qualities such as line, colour and composition, leading the way towards abstraction (see page 400).

Beauty

'Though beauty is seen and confessed by all,' wrote the English painter William Hogarth in 1753, 'yet from the many fruitless attempts to account for the cause of it being so, enquiries on that head have almost been given up ...' Hogarth was commenting on the difficulties of explaining the nature of our experience of works of art.

For centuries, beauty was believed to be an abstract but real quality possessed by certain works of art. Contrary to this position, in 1757 the Scottish philosopher David Hume wrote that 'Beauty is no quality of things themselves. It exists merely in the mind which contemplates them.' This view now broadly predominates, although equal weight is not given to every individual's opinion. We tend to respect the judgement of those who are experts in the field, who can justify their approbation not by identifying some separable quality called 'beauty', nor by telling us about the emotion the work evokes, but by describing the individual work of art itself, and comparing it with others.

The intentional fallacy

In judging a work of art, to what extent should one take into account the context in which the work was created? Do we need to know about medieval theology to understand Dante's *Divine Comedy*, for example, or share his Christian beliefs to fully appreciate his poetry? Does the fact that Richard Wagner was a monster of egotism and a rabid anti-Semite take anything away from the quality of his music?

There are those who say that a work of art can be, and should be, judged entirely on its own merits, and therefore that any knowledge about the beliefs, personality or intentions of the creator is entirely irrelevant. This approach was encouraged in the 1920s by the English literary critic I.A. Richards (1893–1979), whose 'practical criticism' involved presenting his students with the raw texts of poems without any supporting information about the author or the time or place of composition.

The idea of the autonomy of the text was picked up by the American 'New Critics' of the 1940s and 1950s, and in 1946 W.K. Wimsatt and Monroe C. Beardsley published an essay entitled 'The Intentional Fallacy'. In this, they claimed that a poem 'is not the critic's own and not the author's (it is detached from the author at birth and goes about the world beyond his power to intend about it or control it). The poem belongs to the public ...' They conceded that a poem may have an 'intended' meaning, but that this is not the same as the 'actual', independent meaning.

The trouble with this approach is that it isolates the work of art from the circumstances of its production, and so denies that, among other things, a work of art is a historical artefact. Some would say that considering a work of art exclusively as a timeless aesthetic object dishonestly limits the complexity of our responses, and so diminishes our experience.

The affective fallacy

'Take loads of handkerchiefs because you will cry a great deal!' French composer Gabriel Fauré advised a friend setting off for a festival of Wagner operas at Bayreuth in 1884. 'Also take a sedative,' he continued, 'because you will be exalted to the point of delirium!' Others, however, have found that Wagner inspires the most appalling tedium: 'We should prefer a state of perpetual coma,' opined the *London Musical World* in 1855.

Such variations in subjective emotional responses to works of art encouraged the American literary critics W.K. Wimsatt and Monroe C. Beardsley in 1954 to warn against 'a confusion between the poem [or other work of art] and its results (what it is and what it does)'. This 'confusion' they dubbed the 'affective fallacy'. Subsequent critics have found the concept too simplistic; part of the quality of a work of art resides in its ability to elicit a strong emotional response.

Religion

Religion has played a major part in human societies throughout history. But what is religion? We normally think of it as involving a belief in one or more gods. But this is not the case, for example, with Buddhism, in which there are no gods. Like other religions, however, Buddhism does place a strong emphasis on the existence of a spiritual realm, set apart from the everyday material world.

Is someone who claims that they believe in a spiritual realm therefore 'religious'? Not necessarily, because religions are (in part) institutions that embrace a community of people with similar or identical beliefs.

Community is just one aspect of a religion. Others include faith (individual beliefs and feelings of awe and reverence); cult (rituals, sacred buildings, collective worship and so on); creed (doctrines and sacred books); and code (the morals, taboos and ideas about sin and holiness ordained by the religion).

How does religion differ from ideology? Ideologies such as Nazism or communism may, like a religion, require absolute commitment from their followers, and strict adherence to doctrine, but they differ from religions in that they do not include a god or any kind of spiritual dimension.

And how does religion differ from magic? Those who believe in magic hold that certain rituals will bring about the desired changes in the material world, without the intervention of a god. In contrast, within a religion people pray for certain changes, but believe that these will only come about through the intercession of a god.

Religions can also be viewed as cultural phenomena, embodying the value systems and foundation myths of various societies around the world. Some religions, such as Christianity and Islam, lay claim to universality and insist on their unique and special status. Nevertheless, they too can be viewed as products of particular historical circumstances.

Theology

The word 'theology' literally means 'the study of God', and the subject has been defined as an attempt to talk rationally about the divine. Topics include the nature of God, his relationship with the universe and his intentions regarding humanity, the study of sacred texts, and the development of doctrine. All religions have produced some theology, but none more so than Christianity.

There are two main strands in Christian theology – natural and revealed. Natural theology involves deducing knowledge about God from the natural world. The first great proponent of this approach was St Thomas Aquinas (1225–74) who in the 13th century incorporated Aristotelian reasoning into Christian thinking, and came up with a number of arguments for the existence of God (see page 140). Natural theology is now part of Roman Catholic dogma, but is opposed by some who insist that human reason is too corrupted by sin to learn anything about God, who can only be known through divine revelation.

God

God is the supreme being postulated by believers as the creator and ruler of the universe. Most religions either have a single God (monotheism) or many (polytheism), but some, like Buddhism and Daoism, have none.

Polytheistic religions include Hinduism and those of ancient Greece and Rome, but even their pantheons of gods have hierarchies. In Hinduism, for example, the supreme spirit and ultimate reality is Brahman, who operates through the triad of Brahma (the creator), Vishnu (the preserver) and Shiva (the destroyer); in addition, there are numerous other gods, some of them manifestations of the higher gods.

The first monotheistic religion was Judaism; Christianity and Islam – both of which also arose in the Middle East – followed in the same tradition. In Christianity, God is conceived of as a Trinity, comprising Father, Son and Holy Ghost. In the monotheistic religions, God is seen as omnipotent (all-powerful), omniscient (all-knowing) and benevolent (all-loving). He reveals himself in his scriptures – such as the Bible, the Qu'ran and the Torah.

In many religions, God not only created the universe, he is also actively involved in it. This position is known as theism: the theist holds that God is both transcendent (existing above and beyond his creation, outside of time and space) and immanent (actively present and involved in every aspect of his creation).

In contrast, deism – a position adopted by many of the rationalist thinkers of the 18th-century Enlightenment – holds that God was the necessary first cause of the universe (see page 48), but has since withdrawn from involvement.

A different perspective is found in pantheism, which holds that there is no transcendent God – he is only to be found in everything in the universe, including every human being. Although pantheism has been espoused by a number of philosophers such as Baruch Spinoza (1632–77) and Romantic poets such as William Wordsworth, it has never found much acceptance in Western religions.

Arguments for the existence of God

O ver the centuries, a variety of arguments have been proposed in favour of the existence of God. The most prominent of the traditional arguments are outlined below.

1 The cosmological argument. Everything has a cause, and God exists as first cause (see page 48). This can be criticized on the grounds that causality only links observable phenomena.

2 The argument from design. The universe is so complex that it must have been made by an omniscient, omnipotent designer. This presupposes that everything has a purpose (see page 30).

3 The ontological argument. If God is 'that than which nothing greater can be conceived' then he must necessarily exist. This argument is circular.

4 The moral argument. Morality exists, but would not be possible without a just God to ensure that virtue is rewarded.

Faith

As a concept, faith overlaps with, but is not identical to, belief. In philosophy, belief is contrasted with knowledge: when we say we believe something to be the case, we do not have sufficient evidence to say that we know it. Belief in God falls under this category, and this is often what we mean by faith – a strong and unshakable conviction, not requiring proof or evidence.

In Christian theology, faith denotes trust in God, and in his actions and promises. As St Paul put it: 'Now faith is the substance [or 'assurance'] of things hoped for, the evidence of things not seen' (Hebrews 11:1). Faith is regarded as a manifestation of God's grace. A similar idea is found in Islam: 'None can have faith except by the will of Allah' (Qur'an 10:100).

'Natural theologians' hold that the existence of God can wholly or partly be deduced by reason (see pages 136 and 140).

In contrast, 'fideists' hold that religious belief is entirely based on faith. The most extreme version of fideism is encapsulated in the defence of the incarnation made by Tertullian, the 3rd-century Church father: *Certum est quia impossibile est* ('It is certain because it is impossible'). Faith, according to the fideists, is justified by mystical experience, by revelation and by the human need for the irrational.

The relative importance of faith as opposed to 'works' (i.e. good deeds) in determining an individual's salvation has inspired much debate over the centuries. St Paul himself maintained that 'faith without works is dead' (James 2:20).

However, Christian theology maintains that the repentant sinner, if he or she has faith, may be granted salvation by God's grace. This was a particularly important strand in the Protestant Reformation, and Martin Luther expressed it thus: 'Be a sinner and sin strongly, but more strongly have faith and rejoice in Christ.'

Atheism

Atheism is a denial of the existence of God or other spiritual beings. The most common argument in favour of atheism is that there is no evidence that such a being or beings exist. This position broadly coincides with philosophical materialism (see page 64), and has been reinforced by science, which has demonstrated that a divine creator is no longer necessary to explain the observable universe. Various modern philosophers (such as the logical positivists; see page 80) have argued that the concept of God, being untestable, is meaningless. Famously, the German philosopher Friedrich Nietzsche (opposite) proclaimed that 'God is dead.'

Atheism is not the same as agnosticism, which maintains that there is insufficient evidence to conclude whether or not God exists. The question of God's existence, say the agnostics, is simply unanswerable. Strict fideists (see page 142) state that reason has nothing to do with faith, and claim the existence of God is almost by definition unprovable.

Sin

In many societies through history, failure to adhere to social mores and laws, and the violation of taboos, have been regarded not only as wrong, but as a manifestation of spiritual wickedness.

In Judaism, Christianity and Islam, moral evil (see page 104) is characterized as 'sin', and is seen as the deliberate flouting of the will of God. According to Genesis, sin began when Adam and Eve, the first humans, disobeyed God and lost their primal innocence. Ever since then, humans have been born into 'original sin'; in other words, human nature is innately sinful. The so-called 'seven deadly sins' – wrath, greed, sloth, pride, lust, envy and gluttony – are examples of these inherent weaknesses, and are regarded as the origin of 'actual sin'.

Actual sin consists of evil acts – which may be committed in thought, word or deed. Salvation depends (at least in part) on avoiding evil acts by obeying the revealed laws of God (for example the Ten Commandments given by God to Moses). There are sins of omission – failures to carry out one's obligations – as well as sins of commission (see Acts and omissions, page 120).

In Christian doctrine, a distinction is made between mortal and venial sins. Mortal sins involve a deliberate turning away from God and are so serious that they involve total loss of grace, and condemn the sinner to Hell unless the sin is repented.

In the Roman Catholic Church, mortal sins include heresy, murder, adultery, abortion, contraception and perjury. Venial sins are less serious: they are committed with less awareness of wrongdoing, involve only partial loss of grace and are more easily forgiven.

There are also 'formal sins', in which the act is wrong in itself and known by the sinner to be wrong; and 'material sins', in which the act is wrong, but the sinner is not aware of this, and is therefore not held responsible.

Conscience

Conscience is the 'inner voice' that enables us to tell right from wrong. It has variously been attributed to the voice of God or reason, or to some special human faculty – a 'moral sense'. The 18th-century English theologian Joseph Butler (1692–1752) described it as 'a sentiment of the understanding or a perception of the heart'. In Hinduism it is 'the invisible God who dwells within us', while to the Quakers it is the all-important 'inner light' of God.

From non-religious perspectives, individual conscience can be seen to be a result of social and cultural influences. Most societies have moral codes, which are drummed into individuals from an early age. Freudians characterize conscience as the 'superego', a set of inhibitions moulded during childhood by parental approval and disapproval (see page 361). Behaviourists (see page 364) have a similar conception, describing conscience in terms of learned responses to social stimuli – rewards and punishments.

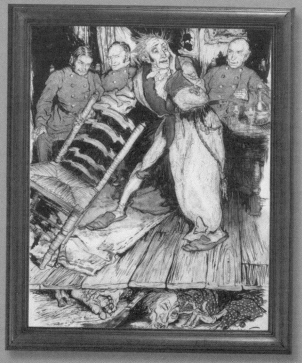

Edgar Allan Poe's short story *The Tell-Tale Heart* tells
the story of a murderer driven mad by guilt, and haunted
by the heartbeat of his victim.

The soul

The idea that each human being has a soul – an immaterial spiritual essence – is common to many cultures and religions, and can be traced to the very beginnings of history.

In ancient Egypt and ancient China, the soul had two aspects, one of which died with the body, while the other survived. In ancient Greece, Aristotle conceived of the soul as a form inseparable from the body (whether of humans, animals or plants). It was in effect the way that the body behaved, the animated aspect of it. In animistic cultures, all living things similarly have a soul, or spirit, as do many inanimate things, such as rocks and rivers.

However, it was the idea of the soul promulgated by another ancient Greek philosopher, Plato, that proved most influential. Plato saw the soul as incorporeal, and only united with the body during life.

This body–soul division was taken up by Christianity, in which the soul is created by God and infused into the body at conception. It survives the death of the body, and at the end of the world it will be subject to divine judgement, and, depending on its merits, assigned either to heaven or hell for eternity (see page 156). Similar beliefs are found in Islam.

In Hinduism and Buddhism, the soul goes through an eternal cycle of reincarnation (see page 154). The nature of each new incarnation depends on *karma*, which can be defined as the consequences of past actions.

The body–soul dichotomy of Christianity lies at the heart of the mind–body dualism promulgated by René Descartes in the 17th century, in which mind and body are two separate substances that nevertheless somehow interact (see page 43).

In modern philosophy, debates about the nature of the soul have become modified into discussions regarding the nature of mind, self, identity and consciousness (see pages 38–43).

Theodicy

If God is omnipotent, omniscient and supremely benevolent, how can he allow evil to exist in the world? What can be the divine purpose behind natural evils such as diseases, earthquakes and floods, or moral evils such as murder, war and poverty?

This is the problem addressed in Christian theology by theodicy, which sets out, in the words of the English poet John Milton at the beginning of *Paradise Lost* (1667), to 'justify the ways of God to men'. Most arguments invoke the idea of free will: God gave humans freedom to choose, and if they choose moral evil, that is their responsibility. This is what happened to Adam and Eve, and their 'original sin' is the origin of all evil, both moral and natural – the latter being a punishment for sin. A rather different argument suggests that the existence of good and evil helps humans to mature, growing towards the perfection for which God designed them.

Reincarnation

Reincarnation is the process by which, after the death of the body, souls are supposedly transported into a different body – sometimes human, sometimes animal and sometimes even vegetable. It is also known as metempsychosis or the transmigration of souls. This is in marked contrast to ideas about the soul and its fate after death propagated in the monotheistic religions (see page 156).

The concept of reincarnation is found in ancient Greek philosophy, in various ancient religions of the Middle East and in some modern mystical movements such as theosophy. However, the concept is most closely associated with religions originating in the Indian subcontinent – Hinduism, Jainism, Sikhism and Buddhism – in which the term *samsara* denotes a continual cycle of birth, death and rebirth.

In these religions, the form in which one is reincarnated depends on *karma* – a word literally meaning 'action', and denoting the idea that one suffers the consequences of one's actions. If one offends by one's actions against *dharma* – variously characterized as 'law', 'way', 'duty' or 'nature' – one will suffer bad *karma*.

In Hinduism, the endless cycle of *samsara* can only be broken if one achieves perfect self-knowledge, involving a realization that the eternal soul or core of the individual and the absolute reality are one and the same. This leads to *moksha*, liberation from the cycle.

In Buddhism, there is no such thing as a permanent 'self' – in fact nothing at all exists permanently. It is only when, through meditation, one detaches oneself from the impermanent and realizes that desire is the cause of all suffering, that one can achieve *nirvana*, or enlightenment, and so escape the cycle of rebirth.

Buddhist philosophers questioned the Hindu conception of reincarnation, asking (as we might) in what sense the reincarnated person counts as the same person as the one who has just died, if the reincarnated person has no memory of their earlier life.

Heaven and hell

Conceptions of heaven and hell – places of either eternal blessedness or eternal punishment – are found in many religions. Heaven may be a place where the virtuous and/or the heroic enjoy a variety of pleasures, or alternatively bask incorporeally in God's love. Similarly, hell may be a place of horrendous physical torments, or it may derive its horror and despair from the absence of God and his love.

Ideas of heaven and hell reflect the very human need to believe in a divinely ordained system of justice – especially given that this commodity often appears to be in short supply here on Earth. Evil men may thrive in their lives, but they will be punished in the hereafter; similarly, the good and the meek may be suffering now, but 'there will be pie in the sky when you die'. Some argue that all this is nothing more than a smokescreen aimed at maintaining social order and preventing people from seeking justice in the here and now.

Prayer and meditation

Prayer is the act of attempting to communicate with a god or gods, or other supernatural powers. Prayer is found in one form or another in most religions, and may be conducted individually or collectively. Some acts of prayer are prescribed in detail, and hence are highly ritualistic, while others are more personalized. Some attempt to bridge the gap between the human and the divine, while others are aimed at bringing out the god within.

Prayer may be aided by a number of techniques and devices. Rosaries or prayer beads are used in several religions as aids to remembering a series of prescribed prayers. Images are sometimes used as focuses of adoration or aids to concentration. In the Roman Catholic and Eastern Orthodox Churches, these are pictures of Christ or various saints, while some forms of Buddhism employ intricate geometrical designs known as mandalas. Both Islam and most Protestant churches regard the use of images in worship as idolatrous.

Prayer has a number of functions. Adoration involves praise of the powers and other attributes of the deity. Petition involves making particular requests, whether for material or spiritual goods, for oneself or for others. Thanksgiving expresses gratitude for the blessings of life – for example, food and good health. Confession involves acknowledging one's deviations from the path of righteousness.

A very particular form of prayer aims at mystical union with the divine. This form of prayer, also known as meditation, involves techniques such as concentration, contemplation and abstraction. In the Christian mystical tradition, the mystical union is described as ecstasy or the beatific vision. There is a similar tradition in Islam, known as Sufism.

In Hinduism and Buddhism, meditation techniques often involve yoga. The aim is to liberate oneself from worldly attachment and so from suffering, and thus achieve enlightenment – release from the cycle of birth, death and rebirth (see page 154).

Predestination

Predestination is the doctrine that God, being omnipotent and omniscient, has foreordained everything that happens. It is important in Christian theology, in which the doctrine specifically states that everyone is predestined either to be saved or damned. The idea arises out of St Paul's Epistle to the Romans (8:29–30): 'For whom he [God] did foreknow, he also did predestinate to be conformed to the image of his Son ... Moreover whom he did predestinate, them he also called: and whom he called, them he also justified: and whom he justified, them he also glorified.'

Predestination is particularly significant in Protestant denominations inspired by the teachings of the French theologian and reformer John Calvin (1509–64). Calvin (opposite) taught that from the beginning of time God has determined whom he will grant salvation, irrespective of their faith, or their love, or how they conduct themselves in life. This idea is not easily squared with free will (see page 50).

Science

Science is the area of human intellectual activity that seeks to provide systematic explanations of what goes on in the physical universe. To stand up, a scientific theory must be comprehensive – it cannot have any exceptions. For example, we would not accept Newton's law of gravity if every now and again boulders shot hundreds of metres into the air from the surface of the Earth. Predictive power is also important – the theory must be testable. For example, the design of an aeroplane's wing means that once the aeroplane reaches a certain speed, we predict that it will rise into the air, as happens on every observed occasion.

The most logically certain theories are those that employ mathematics. From Newton's laws of motion and gravity we can, via mathematical calculations, make deductive inferences (i.e. arguing from the general to the particular) about a whole range of phenomena, from the swing of a pendulum to the timing of the next solar eclipse. Deductive inferences that are not based on mathematics, in contrast, rarely hold water. Not all theories use mathematical concepts: Darwin's theory of evolution by natural selection, for example, has immense explanatory power without resorting to mathematics.

Much science is based on induction, the opposite process to deduction. Induction is the process of deriving general theories from particular empirical evidence, in the form of observations, experiments and measurements. In fact, theories are more typically devised by the scientist's creative imagination. Induction from empirical evidence is then used to justify or refute the theory.

The 18th-century Scottish philosopher David Hume correctly pointed out that there are no *logical* grounds for accepting inductive inferences: no matter how often we observe an aeroplane taking off, there is no *logical* reason why it should do so the next time. Hume conceded that this was not a *practical* point. In practice, we accept theories if they are backed up by sufficient empirical evidence.

Mathematics

Mathematics is the study of number, quantity, shape and space, and their interrelationships. Applied maths uses mathematical techniques to help to understand physical and technological processes (see page 162). Pure maths is entirely abstract – it does not depend on what happens in the physical world, or indeed on anything outside itself. The truth of a mathematical theory depends on logic and rigorous formal proof, not on experiment.

A mathematical theory is presented in the form of a series of axioms – statements or formulae that are held to be true, and from which the whole theory can be deduced. In the early 20th century, mathematicians believed that their subject could be shown to be a complete and self-consistent system. However, in 1931 the Austrian logician Kurt Gödel demolished this hope when he proved that in a mathematical system based on a finite number of axioms there will always be some propositions that are true but cannot be proved from the axioms.

$$\beta = \frac{1}{\sqrt{1 - \frac{V^2}{C^2}}}$$

$$1 = \frac{1}{2}$$

$$x + 3 = 5$$

$$x(x-1) = x^2 - 1$$

$$8 = 2 \cdot x \quad y = yx^2 \quad \frac{1}{2P_0} \qquad 52 - x^2 + y = ?$$

$$9 - y = 7$$

$$\sqrt{64}$$

$$y \int B \cdot dA = 0$$

$$MC = x^2$$

$$\sum_{N} \frac{\partial^2 v_{z,2}}{\partial t^2} - C_s^2 \frac{\partial^2 v_2^2}{\partial z^2} =$$

Paradigm shifts

In his 1962 book *The Structure of Scientific Revolutions*, the American philosopher and historian Thomas S. Kuhn suggested that science develops not in a continuous and linear way, but rather through a series of 'paradigm shifts'.

In the philosophy of science, a paradigm is a very general world-view, a conceptual framework within which scientists operate, and within which any particular investigation is undertaken. Within a given paradigm, researchers carry on 'normal science', solving puzzles thrown up by the existing world-view, but not seeking to challenge it.

A paradigm shift is a scientific revolution during which one paradigm replaces another. This leads to a period of 'revolutionary science' in which new perspectives are opened up, new lines of inquiry present themselves and new questions are asked about old data and old assumptions. Paradigm shifts typically occur when the inconsistencies and unsolvable puzzles that are thrown up by the existing paradigm accumulate to such an extent that it is stretched to breaking point.

The classic example of a paradigm shift is the realization by Nicolaus Copernicus (1473–1543) that the ancient Ptolemaic Earth-centred model of the universe could not explain numerous accumulated observations of the planets. Hypothesizing that the Earth orbited the Sun, and not vice versa, he found that his new model fitted the data far better. Copernicus' Sun-centred model was virulently denounced by the Roman Catholic Church, as it removed the Earth, and thus humanity, from the centre of the universe. Other examples of paradigm shifts include the overthrow of Newtonian mechanics by quantum physics and relativity in the early 20th century (see pages 182–4).

In shining a light on paradigm shifts, and the fact that different paradigms are often incompatible, Kuhn showed that science, rather then being the entirely objective pursuit it is widely thought to be, is in fact a human activity. As such, science is to a certain degree subjective, shaped as it is by social, cultural and historical factors.

Space

Space is conventionally defined as the boundless expanse in which all objects are located. Within the framework of space, the positions of all objects relative to each other can be given by distance and direction. Space, one of the fundamental quantities of science, is measured by the metre. According to Newtonian mechanics (see page 178), space has three linear dimensions and is absolute, existing independently of any matter within it. According to the theory of relativity (see page 184), space is just part of the continuum of space-time, with time being the fourth dimension. What is more, relativity tells us that space-time is not absolute – both of its aspects can be distorted by gravitational fields around massive objects.

The widely supported Big Bang theory (see page 188) posits that space-time came into being 13.7 billion years ago, since when it has been expanding continuously. In the abstract, space is conceived of as limitless, but whether the universe itself is infinite is a question that continues to exercise cosmologists.

According to general relativity, space-time acts
like a multi-dimensional 'rubber sheet' that can
be distorted by the presence of large masses.

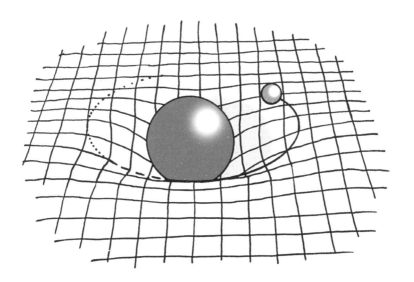

Time

Time is one of the fundamental quantities of physics. It measures duration, usually in relation to some regular periodic process such as the rotation of the Earth or the emission of radiation by caesium atoms (used as the basis for the modern definition of the second, the fundamental unit of time).

Our subjective experience of time suggests that it is not absolute – time drags when we are bored and rushes along when we are enjoying ourselves. From our point of view, past, present and future overlap – we are always aware of more than an infinitely small 'now', pondering what has happened and anticipating what is about to occur.

Contrary to this experience, though, classical Newtonian mechanics insists that time passes at a uniform rate. However, Einstein's theories of relativity (see page 184) tells us that time is *not* absolute, and that at speeds approaching that of light (relative to the observer) time is dilated. Together with space, time forms the four-dimensional continuum called space-time.

Time can be defined as the framework within which change occurs. It also appears to have direction: although most laws of physics allow processes to go in both directions, some do not. An example is the second law of thermodynamics, formulated in the 19th century, which dictates that the entropy (disorder or chaos) of any system increases with time. Rocks crumble, cars rust, living things die and decay – all irreversible processes.

According to the Big Bang theory (see page 188), the universe began 13.7 billion years ago. If time existed before this, then whatever happened in this earlier time-frame could have had no effect upon the present time-frame.

Will time go on for ever? The second law of thermodynamics suggests that all motion and thus all change – and time itself – will eventually cease. However, some cosmologists suggest that our universe is just one of myriad such universes in a so-called 'multiverse'.

Infinity

Infinity is any quantity – either very large or very small – without end or limit. It is one of those concepts that it is difficult for the human mind to grasp, particularly in relation to time and space. It is nigh-on impossible to imagine 'forever', and yet the notion of a boundary of space or an end of time is equally imponderable: we always end up asking what is beyond the edge, or what happens after the end of time. Physicists and cosmologists have yet to come up with conclusive answers.

In mathematics, the concept of infinitesimals – quantities that are infinitely small, but greater than zero – is essential to the calculus developed in the late 17th century. Two centuries later, the German mathematician Georg Cantor (1845–1918) showed that the set of all the natural (i.e. counting) numbers appears to be larger than the set of just the even natural numbers. There are thus different infinities, some of which are larger than others.

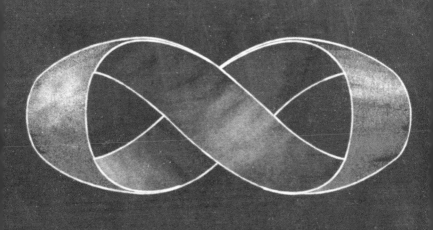

Matter

Matter is any substance – solid, liquid or gas – that occupies space and has mass. Although the ancient Greeks came up with their own atomic theory of matter (see page 64), the modern atomic theory began in the early 19th century when English chemist John Dalton (1766–1844) proposed that homogenous substances are made up of tiny identical particles called atoms. These are essentially indivisible and remain unchanged during chemical reactions.

Dalton did not distinguish between atoms and molecules. Atoms are the basic units of elements (hydrogen, oxygen, iron, gold, uranium, etc.), and differ in mass and chemical properties depending on the element concerned. Molecules (which are composed of more than one atom, usually of different elements) are the basic units of chemical compounds. For example, a water molecule has two atoms of hydrogen and one of oxygen.

At the end of the 19th century, the English physicist J.J. Thomson (1856–1940) discovered the electron, a tiny negatively charged particle within the atom. This showed that atoms *are* divisible, and sparked off intensive research into atomic structure. The model that emerged pictures the atom as largely empty space, in which a minute nucleus is surrounded by 'clouds' of negatively charged electrons. The nucleus contains most of the atom's mass and consists of protons (particles with a positive charge) and neutrons (which have no charge). Further research on fundamental particles led to the 'standard model' of particle physics (see page 186).

Our assumptions about the nature of matter were further weakened by quantum theory (see page 182), which, among other concepts, introduces the idea that electrons and various other particles can behave like waves. Another assumption, that matter can neither be created nor destroyed, was demolished when Einstein came up with his formula $E = mc^2$ (see pages 184–5). This shows that matter is convertible into energy and vice versa, as demonstrated by nuclear fission and nuclear fusion, the basis of nuclear weapons and nuclear power.

Wave theory

Although we primarily think of waves as undulations in a body of water, many physical phenomena – from sound to light to X-rays – are actually made up of waves. A wave is any periodic change or oscillation that is propagated through a medium or space. Most transport energy from one place to another – for example, sound waves transfer mechanical energy, while light waves transfer electromagnetic energy (see page 180). In transverse waves, the oscillations are at right

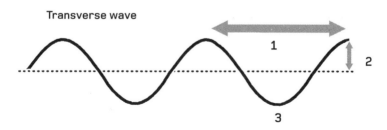

Transverse wave

angles to the direction of travel, while in longitudinal waves they are parallel to the direction of travel.

All waves have three characteristics in common: amplitude, wavelength and frequency (see below). Waves can be reflected (bounced off a surface), refracted (bent by passage through another medium) and diffracted (spread out after passing through a small gap). They can also interfere with each other. Whatever the type of wave, all these characteristics can be described using similar mathematical formulae.

1 Wavelength: distance between successive wave peaks or troughs
2 Amplitude: height of waves or magnitude of disturbance

3 Frequency: number of peaks or troughs passing a fixed point in a second

Longitudinal wave

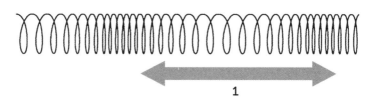

Newtonian mechanics

Mechanics is the branch of physics that describes the motion of objects, whether at the galactic or the sub-atomic scale. Most types of motion – from the orbit of a planet to the trajectory of a cannonball – can be described by the three laws of motion and the law of gravitation formulated by the great English physicist and mathematician, Sir Isaac Newton (1642–1727).

Underlying Newton's laws is the concept of force. A force is anything that alters the rate of change of the velocity of a body. This rate of change may involve acceleration or deceleration in a uniform direction, or it may involve a change in the direction of motion.

Newton's first law of motion states that a body will remain at rest or travelling in a straight line and at a constant speed unless acted upon by some external force. The tendency of a body to remain at rest or move at a constant velocity is its inertia, and this depends on the mass of the body.

Newton's second law states that the force acting on a body is equal to the change created in its momentum (the product of its mass and its velocity). The third law states that every action force is balanced by an equal and opposite reaction.

Newton's law of gravitation states that every mass in the universe exerts a force on every other mass, and that this force is directly proportional to the product of their masses and inversely proportional to the square of the distance between them. Gravity itself is one of the fundamental forces of nature and is only partly understood.

Newton's laws have proved enormously successful in their predictive power and in their practical applications. However, relativity (see page 184) and quantum theory (see page 182) respectively show that they apply neither at velocities approaching the speed of light, nor at the subatomic scale.

Electromagnetism

Magnetism and electricity were poorly understood until
early in the 19th century, when a series of experiments
showed that an electric current flowing through a copper
wire affected the needles of nearby magnetic compasses. It
became clear that both magnetism and electricity were forces
that could act on each other at a distance. In 1831, English
physicist Michael Faraday (1791–1867) demonstrated that an
electric current is induced in a wire if subjected to a changing
magnetic field. This is the basis of the electrical generator,
while the opposite process is the basis of the electric motor.

Later in the 19th century, Scottish physicist James Clerk
Maxwell (1831–79) proposed that electricity and magnetism
were manifestations of a single electromagnetic force and
that electrical oscillations would generate electromagnetic
waves. Further research validated his theories, and it was
discovered that all sorts of phenomena, from radio waves
through visible light to X-rays, are electromagnetic in nature.

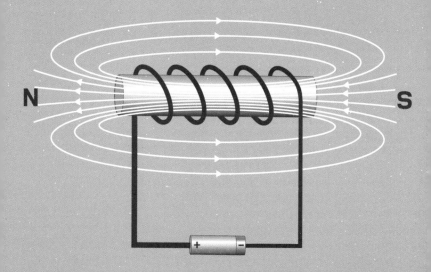

An electromagnet consists of a conducting wire
coiled around an iron core. When current flows
through the wire, a magnetic field is induced within
and around the core.

Quantum theory

Towards the end of the 19th century, observations of various phenomena relating to electromagnetic radiation raised questions that classical physics seemed incapable of answering. Then in 1900 the German physicist Max Planck suggested that electromagnetic radiation – including light – is not emitted as a continuous wave, but as discrete bundles of energy called quanta. Planck linked the energy (E) of each quantum to the frequency of the wave (f) in the equation $E = hf$, where h is the so-called Planck constant.

One of the more puzzling phenomena was the photoelectric effect, in which electrons are emitted when light or other forms of electromagnetic radiation strike certain metals. In 1905, Albert Einstein proposed that the effect could only be explained if Planck's quantum theory of light was correct. In the case of the photoelectric effect, light behaves not as a wave, but as a stream of particles (now known as photons). Two decades later, the French physicist Louis Victor de

Broglie (1892–1987) suggested that electrons display a similar 'wave-particle duality'.

Planck's idea prompted the Danish physicist Niels Bohr to suggest in 1913 that inside the atom (see page 175), electrons can only move in certain permitted orbits, each with its own energy level. When an electron jumps from a higher to a lower energy level, radiation is released in discrete quanta.

In 1927, the German physicist Werner Heisenberg devised his famous uncertainty principle. Newtonian mechanics (see page 178) assumes that the position and momentum of a body can be measured simultaneously with infinite accuracy. The uncertainty principle states that at the atomic and subatomic scale, this is not possible, because the very act of observing alters the outcome.

Quantum theory, undermining as it does many conceptual frameworks such as causality, may seem contrary to common sense. But it has been found to have innumerable practical applications, not least in our understanding of semiconductors, the basis of modern computing technology.

Relativity

Newtonian mechanics holds that mass, space and time are all absolute. For virtually all practical purposes these assumptions work perfectly well, but Albert Einstein's special theory (1905) and general theory (1915) of relativity proposed that in certain circumstances Newtonian mechanics no longer apply.

The special theory of relativity states that nothing can travel faster than the speed of light, which in a vacuum is constant, regardless of the motion of the observer. If an object passes rapidly by an observer, it will appear to have become shorter and more massive – although this effect is only significant at speeds approaching the speed of light. Likewise, a clock passing at similar speeds relative to the observer will appear to be running slower than when it is at rest. The general theory proposes the idea of space-time (see page 168), and states that mass can 'bend' both space and light via gravity. Experiments have subsequently validated Einstein's theories.

$$E = mc^2$$

Einstein's famous equation shows that energy (E)
is equal to mass (m) multiplied by the square of the
speed of light (c).

The standard model and string theory

The standard model of particle physics has been described as 'the theory of almost everything'. It concerns three of the four fundamental forces of nature, and uses quantum mechanics to describe the ways that these forces affect subatomic particles.

Building on earlier models of the atom (see page 175), from the middle of the 20th century theoretical physicists proposed a wide range of subatomic particles. These explained a variety of experimental results, and the existence of many of these hypothetical particles has subsequently been established. For example, in 1964 the American physicist Murray Gell-Mann proposed that the protons and neutrons found in atomic nuclei are each made of three even smaller particles, which he called quarks. These have since been discovered.

Quarks, which come in a number of 'flavours' and 'colours', are a class of elementary particle. They are held together by the strong nuclear force, which is mediated by the exchange of particles called gluons. Gluons are a type of gauge boson, a class of elementary particle that mediates the fundamental forces. The weak nuclear force, which is involved in certain types of radioactivity, is mediated by W and Z bosons, while the electromagnetic force is mediated by photons. The electromagnetic force causes the interaction between electrically charged particles, such as protons and electrons. Electrons belong to the third class of elementary particle, the leptons. Other leptons include the neutrino, which has no charge and virtually no mass.

The standard model does not accommodate the fourth fundamental force, gravitation, which is governed by general relativity (see page 184). Incorporating it would require the existence of a fourth gauge boson, the graviton, but this particle remains hypothetical. One attempt to reconcile quantum mechanics and general relativity into a 'theory of everything' is string theory, which suggests that electrons and quarks are oscillating one-dimensional 'strings'. String theory remains controversial since it requires unobserved additional dimensions and has yet to make any testable predictions.

The Big Bang

In 1929, the American astronomer Edwin Hubble observed that various galaxies are not only moving away from us, but that the further away they are, the faster they are receding. This gave rise to the idea that the universe is expanding, and that it must have originated in a massive 'Big Bang' – now generally agreed to have taken place 13.7 billion years ago.

At the beginning, the universe was very small, very dense and very hot, and made up of the simplest elementary particles. Expansion was phenomenally rapid, and within a matter of minutes, protons and neutrons had come together to form the nuclei of hydrogen and helium that began to coalesce into stars, within which other elements were soon being created. Expansion has continued ever since, but whether it will go on forever is unknown. If the universe has sufficient mass, its gravity may eventually pull it back into a 'Big Crunch' (perhaps leading to another Big Bang event). If not, then expansion will continue forever, and the universe will suffer a long cold death.

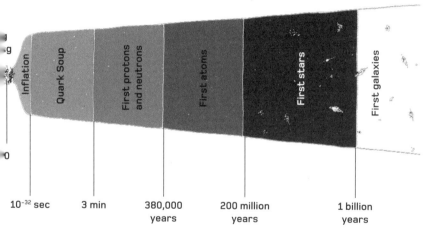

The first billion years
of cosmic history

Inflation

Quark Soup

First protons
and neutrons

First atoms

First stars

First galaxies

10^{-32} sec   3 min   380,000
years   200 million
years   1 billion
years

Chaos theory

Chaos theory is an area of mathematics that studies how small differences in initial conditions within complex dynamic systems can result in widely different outcomes. Chaos theory has been applied to systems in a range of fields, including meteorology, biology and physics. Although such systems are deterministic (see page 46), with no random elements, the *apparently* chaotic way that they behave makes prediction very difficult.

An early pioneer of chaos theory was the American mathematician and meteorologist Edward Lorenz. In 1961 Lorenz was using a computer model to predict the weather. He started by inputting data relating to such interdependent variables as temperature, humidity, air pressure and the strength and direction of the wind. The first time he ran the program, he typed in a figure of .506127 for one of the variables. Then, when he ran the program again, he took a short cut, typing in the rounded figure of .506. The weather scenario that resulted the second time was completely different from the first. The tiny disparity of .000127 had had a huge effect.

In 1963 one of Lorenz's colleagues remarked that if he was right, 'one flap of a seagull's wings would be enough to alter the weather forever'. In 1972, in the title of a paper, Lorenz asked 'Does the flap of a butterfly's wings in Brazil set off a tornado in Texas?' Thus chaos theory found its popular name: the butterfly effect. Of course, the flap of a single butterfly's wings does not cause the tornado on its own – numerous other factors play their part. But that one flap can be (to change the metaphor) the straw that breaks the camel's back.

Despite its name, chaos theory is rigorously mathematical and has helped to elucidate the hidden order that underlies a host of apparently random systems – from the factors precipitating epileptic fits to the air turbulence that causes drag in moving vehicles, and from fluctuations in wild animal populations to the flow of traffic on congested city streets.

Artificial intelligence

In 1950, the English mathematician Alan Turing suggested a test to establish whether a machine could be called intelligent. A human sitting in one room asks questions of another human in a second room, and of a computer in a third room. If the human in the first room cannot judge whether he or she is talking to a human or a machine, then the computer has passed the so-called 'Turing test'.

Doubts have been cast on the validity of this test. In a famous thought experiment, a man sits in a room while people outside the room slide questions in Chinese under the door. The man does not understand Chinese, but follows a set of instructions that tell him what pieces of paper to push back under the door. As a result, people outside the room cannot tell that he is not a native Chinese speaker. The conclusion is that even when computers can be made to give the right answers, they still cannot ever be conscious, intelligent minds.

In the Turing test, a human questioner **(1)** sends questions to another room, where they are answered by a human volunteer **(2)**, and a computer **(3)**. The experiment controller **(4)** decides at random which of the two answers the questioner will receive.

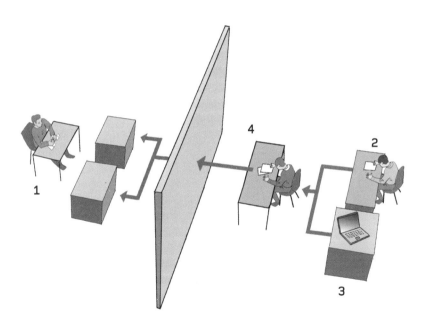

Germ theory

For centuries, the causes of many diseases remained a mystery. Some blamed disease on poison, some on bad air, some on God's displeasure. In the 1840s Ignaz Semmelweiss, a Hungarian obstetrician working in Vienna, noted that women in labour attended by doctors were much more likely to succumb to puerperal fever (usually with fatal results) than those attended by midwives. He made the connection that the doctors had often come straight from autopsies without washing their hands, and insisted that the doctors disinfect themselves before examining their patients. Semmelweiss's ideas aroused much hostility and were generally ignored at the time.

In the 1850s, during an outbreak of cholera in London, the physican John Snow mapped the incidence of cases and showed that the highest density was among people who used a particular pump to obtain drinking water. Snow removed the pump's handle and the number of cases declined dramatically.

These connections helped to show how diseases spread. Some had begun to suggest that the causative agents might be germs – micro-organisms only visible through a microscope. It was left to the French microbiologist Louis Pasteur (1822–95) to find ways of preventing and treating diseases caused by micro-organisms. He used heating to destroy harmful micro-organisms in milk, and developed vaccines to cure both rabies and anthrax. The German physician Robert Koch (1843–1910) also played a pivotal role, identifying the bacteria that cause diseases such as cholera and tuberculosis, and setting out the criteria for establishing whether a disease is caused by a micro-organism.

The acceptance of the germ theory of disease justified Semmelweiss's insistence on cleanliness, and in the 1870s the British surgeon Joseph Lister pioneered antiseptic surgery. The next great breakthrough was the discovery of penicillin by the Scottish microbiologist Alexander Fleming in 1928. This was the first of many antibiotics, drugs that have proved effective against a great range of bacterial diseases, saving millions of lives.

Evolution

The theory of evolution by natural selection outlined by the English naturalist Charles Darwin in *The Origin of Species* (1859) is one of the simplest and most elegant theories in science. It also transformed the way that we think about ourselves (see pages 30, 32, 122, 242 and 366).

Darwin spent decades accumulating and ordering his evidence before publishing his theory. Geologists had shown that the

Earth was very much older than previously imagined, and that the ancient rocks preserved fossils of many animals that are now extinct. Comparing these fossils with each other, and similar but different living species, Darwin suggested that groups of similar modern species had evolved by small gradations from common ancestors. The mechanism he suggested was natural selection. Every now and again a chance mutation arises in an individual that happens to make it better suited to its environment. Such individuals are thus more likely to breed successfully, and so pass on the adaptation. It is in this way that new species – including ourselves – arise.

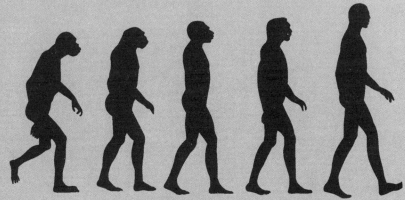

Nature vs nurture

What Darwin did not know when he developed his theory of evolution by natural selection (see page 196) was how new adaptations and other characteristics are passed from one generation to the next. Ironically, during Darwin's lifetime an Austrian monk called Gregor Mendel (1822–84) found the answer, but his results were published in an obscure journal and were forgotten for many years.

Prior to Mendel's discovery of the laws of inheritance, it was assumed that any one characteristic inherited by an offspring was a blend of the characteristics of the parents. Through his experiments with generations of pea plants, Mendel demonstrated that any one characteristic, such as flower colour, is inherited from *either* the male *or* the female parent. The unit that passes on this characteristic is called a gene.

The next great breakthrough came in 1953 when the American James Watson and the Englishman Francis Crick demonstrated *how* genes transmit characteristics. The key is a complex molecule called DNA, found in every cell of every living organism. The DNA of every organism (apart from clones) is unique, containing the code for the way in which that particular individual will grow and develop.

One question that arises is whether DNA determines *everything* about the way that an organism will behave. If it does, this raises further questions relating to determinism, free will and whether there is such a thing as human nature (see pages 20, 46 and 50) – questions that in turn have political implications.

Evolutionary psychologists assert that much behaviour is determined (see page 366), but cognitive psychologists point out the important role of learning (see page 368), while sociologists and anthropologists insist on the key parts played by society and culture in determining how individuals will turn out. The overall scientific consensus seems to be that both genetic inheritance *and* environment – both nature and nurture – shape the way we are.

Politics

Politics has been described both as an art and as a science. The word itself has been variously defined. It can refer to the study and the practice of creating, leading and administering states or other political units. It also includes the relationships between individuals within a society, especially relationships involving power and authority. As an activity, it may involve the mobilization of political parties, development of policies, campaigning, and the formation of governments. To some degree or another it involves compromise and a striving towards consensus.

Politics has famously been characterized as 'the art of the possible', a perspective that goes back to Aristotle, who saw politics as the art of controlling and reconciling the wide range of interests within a state. This most closely conforms with what happens in democracies, but even in highly authoritarian states, some degree of juggling may be required on the part of the rulers.

As a subject for intellectual study, 'political thought' or 'political science' encompasses theories of the state, government, sovereignty, law, the relationships between ruler and ruled, methods of representation and so on. It also covers the descriptive and comparative study of political institutions such as constitutions, parliaments and voting systems. In addition, there are deeper, more philosophical approaches, in which the fundamental values underlying political discourse – such as justice, authority, equality and liberty – are subjected to critical scrutiny.

Political beliefs and values manifest themselves in a range of ideologies and political movements, ranging from single-issue platforms such as pacifism, to totalitarian systems such as fascism or communism. In between are a broad range of political traditions, such as conservatism, liberalism and democratic socialism, each of which present a number of policies embodying aspects of their visions of society, the economy and so on. The political scientist may study such ideologies and movements from a variety of perspectives, whether economic, sociological, historical or philosophical.

The state

A state – in contrast to civil society (see page 214) – is a formally constituted association of persons with a system of laws and a government with the power to enforce them within a demarcated territory. The state is in some ways like a person: it is regarded – popularly and in international law – as responsible for its actions, and as having rights and obligations. Over time, a state acquires something like a personal identity – and, indeed, states are often personified in figures such as Uncle Sam (opposite) or John Bull.

The state can be seen as a voluntary association of individuals coming together for their mutual benefit; this is the idea of the social contract (see page 212). Alternatively, it can be seen in terms of power, as the monopolization and legitimization of violence within a given territory. For Marxists, it is specifically an institution that emerges at a certain stage of economic development in order to protect capitalist production.

Government

Government is the institution that controls individuals and society as a whole, usually within the framework of a state (see page 202). It normally does this via the promulgation and enforcement of laws.

Nearly all modern states have some form of constitution – a collection of fundamental laws that define and limit the powers of government, and that outline the rights of the individual (see page 210). The effectiveness of such checks on a government's untrammelled powers varies; redress is usually available, at least notionally, through the courts.

At different times and in different places various classifications of government have been made. In ancient Greece, Aristotle identified five types: monarchy (literally, 'rule by one', but in the interests of the many); tyranny (in which a single person rules solely in his or her own interest); aristocracy (literally, 'rule by the best', selected, according to

Aristotle, on the basis of virtue, and ruling in the interests of the many); oligarchy (literally, 'rule by a few', selected on the basis of wealth, and ruling in their own interests); and democracy (literally, 'rule by the people').

There are still plenty of examples around the world of tyrannies, in the form of elected or unelected dictators, and informal oligarchies still hold sway in certain countries. The modern version of Aristotle's 'aristocracy' would be meritocracy – in which the most capable people wield power. This may apply to civil servants, but not necessarily to elected politicians. To Aristotle's list one might add theocracy, which literally means 'government by God', and denotes a country – such as Afghanistan under the Taliban – in which religious leaders play a dominant role.

Today, where monarchs do survive, they are mostly no more than ceremonial figureheads. Democracy is now (nominally at least) the commonest form of government (see page 228) around the world, and most countries are republics, with an elected president, rather than a monarch, as head of state.

Sovereignty

Sovereignty, in the sense of supreme power, has two aspects. In international law, a sovereign state is one that is internationally recognized as having unrestricted power within its own borders. However, a nation's sovereignty may be compromised, for example, by its membership of supranational bodies such as the European Union. States may also come into conflict if rivals claim sovereignty over a particular territory.

Within a state, the question arises as to where sovereignty resides. Formerly, in European monarchies, sovereignty was seen to reside in the sovereign, although in fact there were often disputes with the Roman Catholic Church over jurisdiction in religious or spiritual matters.

In Britain, as parliamentary democracy developed, there emerged the idea that legal sovereignty resides in 'the king (or queen) in Parliament', although de facto power over executive decision-making is held by the cabinet of the day. In the USA, internal sovereignty is vested in the Constitution (see page 211).

Law

The possession of a system of laws is one of the most important attributes of a state. Laws are generally intended to apply to all citizens equally, and their very existence limits the powers of the rulers over the ruled. In ancient Greece, for example, the growth in literacy combined with the public display of the laws circumscribed the traditional power of the nobility and helped to usher in democracy.

In theory at least, the law, considered collectively, is supposed to embody justice, and to implement it – although this is not to say that there is no such thing as an unjust law. In order to ensure the carriage of justice, judges are meant to be neutral, and courts of law are generally open to the press and the public, so that justice can not only be done, but also be *seen* to be done.

In Western countries, there are two main systems of law. Roman law, practised widely in continental Europe, derives from that of ancient Rome. It is based on certain general codes (such as the Napoleonic Code promulgated in France and various other countries at the beginning of the 19th century). It employs an inquisitorial system, in which the judge or magistrate investigates the case and questions witnesses in court prior to coming to a verdict.

In contrast, common law, employed in the USA, Britain and many Commonwealth countries, is based not on statutes passed by Congress or Parliament, but on judicial precedent, in which an earlier judgement is regarded as binding on all similar cases.

Such precedent can only be overturned by statute or by a higher court. In common-law systems, court proceedings are adversarial: lawyers for each side argue their case before a judge. The verdict is either delivered by the judge, or in certain cases by a jury – a randomly selected group of citizens whose role is to consider the evidence and come to a reasonable conclusion about the case.

Constitutionalism

Most countries have a written constitution – a group of fundamental laws that define and limit the powers of government, set out how the government is elected, and list the rights of the individual citizen. Constitutional government is intended to embody political liberty, and to represent the will of the people.

Constitutional thinking was developed in the 17th and 18th centuries, emerging through the idea of the social contract (see page 212). Great Britain was one of the first countries to establish a constitutional monarchy (in which the monarch's powers are limited by the will of Parliament), but unusually it does not have a written constitution. The first important written constitution was that of the United States, developed in the 1780s. This established a series of checks and balances between people, state governments and the federal government, and established the principle of the separation of powers, now found in most constitutions.

The social contract

The idea of the social contract lies behind most constitutional thinking. In the social contract, the people surrender their liberties and their sovereignty to a government, whose role it is to establish and maintain social order, via the rule of law.

The English philosopher Thomas Hobbes developed his version of the social contract amid the chaos of the English Civil War. In his 1651 treatise *Leviathan*, Hobbes described human life in the natural, ungoverned state as 'solitary, poor, nasty, brutish and short'. Hobbes believed that people could only live together in peace if they agreed to obey an absolute sovereign.

Later in the same century, another English philosopher, John Locke, rejected absolutism in his *Second Treatise on Government* (1690). This was written in the immediate wake of the 'Glorious Revolution', in which the English overthrew one king with absolutist tendencies (James II) in favour of another

(William III) who promised to uphold the rights and liberties of the people. Locke argued that legitimate government can only exist where it has the consent of the governed. Although the latter surrender their 'natural rights' in agreeing to be governed, they in return are entitled to certain civil rights. If the government fails to uphold these rights, and no longer governs for the good of the governed, the people have the right to change their government. This radical idea had a powerful influence on the instigators of the American Revolution of 1776.

The third version – which influenced the French Revolutionaries of 1789 – was that described by the French philosopher Jean-Jacques Rousseau in *The Social Contract* (1762). Rousseau developed the idea of 'popular sovereignty', arguing that citizens can only be bound by the laws if they play a part in making them. Government should at all times accord with the 'general will', and the individual must bow to this will. Rousseau's version of the social contact was subsequently hijacked by those of a totalitarian tendency, particularly on the left, to justify the suppression of individual liberties.

Civil society

Civil society comprises all those institutions within a state that are independent of the government. Such institutions include a wide range of bodies – from voluntary organizations and social and sports clubs, to protest groups and church congregations – where individuals come together by mutual agreement and free association. Civil society is sometimes distinguished from 'society' more generally, in that it has a political aspect, denoting those bodies that carry out collective actions without the sanction of the state.

The development of civil society is often regarded as a key requisite of democracy. In contrast, totalitarianism (see page 226) cannot tolerate it – all activities must be controlled by the state. Civil societies have re-emerged in many former communist countries, although in China the phenomenon is still embryonic and endangered. Even in established democracies, debates continue over which things should be the responsibility of the state, and what should be left to civil society.

Violence

The commandment 'Thou shalt not kill' is generally accepted – in law as well as in moral codes – as the strongest of the injunctions handed down by God to Moses, as recorded in the Old Testament and perpetuated in all the monotheistic religions. The injunction seems to recognize a propensity of humans to do the opposite unless somehow constrained.

The 17th-century English philosopher Thomas Hobbes certainly believed this to be the case, suggesting that before humans gathered together to form states, they lived in continual fear of violent death. Hobbes believed that the primary duty of government is to preserve life, and in most legal systems violence perpetrated by private citizens is a crime. There are areas where consensus has proved elusive – for example, the arguments over abortion and euthanasia.

In contrast to a general prohibition on the individual acting violently, the state generally reserves the right to carry out acts of violence itself. In some countries, corporal and/ or capital punishment is sanctioned by the law, defended on grounds such as deterrence and/or justice (see punishment, page 348). War is also sanctioned – both in national and international law – in certain circumstances (see page 220). In opposition to this, complete pacifism is only espoused by small minorities (see page 222).

Over the centuries, various political theorists have defended the use of violence to change an intolerable state of affairs. The American Revolutionaries of 1776 used the social-contract arguments of John Locke (see page 212) to justify rebellion, while for Karl Marx and his followers, the revolutionary overthrow of capitalism and the social injustice it perpetuates, is both desirable and inevitable (see page 260).

Marxists also espouse the concept of 'structural violence' – the notion that the state is implicitly violent in that it defends its existence, and the continuation of injustice, by means of its police force and its armed services. In this context, violent resistance is seen to be justified.

Deterrence

Deterrence is the doctrine that if a country has sufficiently strong armed forces, and a mighty arsenal of weaponry, no other country will dare to attack it, or to endanger its interests. This is generally the justification any country puts forward for spending huge sums on 'defence', in the hope that if it does so, it will never need to fight a war.

The trouble with this doctrine is that it leads to arms races, which serve to increase tensions and mutual fear. In the Cold War, the doctrine of deterrence evolved into that of 'mutually assured destruction' (MAD for short), which held that neither side would launch a first nuclear strike, because they knew that the other side would be able to respond with a devastating retaliation. The development of anti-ballistic missile systems has always threatened to disturb this delicate 'balance of terror', since such systems might enable one side to survive a retaliatory strike.

War

War is widely regarded as evil, and yet history is littered with wars that have been justified by their perpetrators on moral or legal grounds. Such arguments presuppose that it is right to commit evil acts in order to counter an even greater evil. This accords with the consequentialist view of ethics, that ends may justify means, but is at odds with the deontological, and pacifist, view that moral injunctions such as 'Thou shalt not kill' are absolute and apply in all circumstances (see page 118).

The idea of the 'just war' was developed by the Roman Catholic Church in the Middle Ages and is now incorporated into international law. 'Just cause' is the most crucial – and the most debatable – condition for a war being regarded as just. Defence against territorial aggression is widely accepted, but other 'just causes' are more controversial. These include religious or ideological motives, pre-emptive action against potential aggression, and action taken to protect overseas economic interests.

Another condition is 'right intention', i.e. that the reason for fighting the war is the rectification of the wrong stated in the just cause. The concept of 'proper authority' states that only an internationally recognized sovereign state can authorize military action; however, this fails to address a variety of circumstances where some might believe military action is justified, for example, where a brutally repressed population rebels against unjust rule.

War must always be regarded as a last resort, after such things as diplomacy and economic sanctions have failed, and the conduct of the war must be proportional to the wrong it sets out to rectify.

In addition, there are international laws, such as the Geneva Conventions, that seek to moderate the conduct of war – for example, by awarding protection to civilians and prisoners of war. Breaches of any of the laws of war may be treated as war crimes and punished accordingly.

Pacifism

Pacifism is the belief that killing humans – and all other forms of violence – is absolutely wrong in all circumstances. A pacifist is not necessarily the same as someone who protests against a particular war; the latter might well believe that some wars are justifiable. In many instances, pacifism is rooted in religious belief: all Quakers, for example, are pacifists, as are many Buddhists. Most Christian denominations, however, and most Muslims, believe in the idea of 'just war' (see page 220).

Although pacifists are sometimes mocked as woolly-minded idealists, non-violence has often proved a successful tactic in politics. In India's struggle for independence from British rule in the first half of the 20th century, Mahatma Gandhi (1869–1948) advocated non-violent civil disobedience – an approach that proved highly influential, for example, in the campaigns led by Martin Luther King (1929–68) to obtain civil rights for African Americans in the 1950s and 1960s.

Absolutism

There have always been rulers who have attempted to wield absolute power, but the notion of absolute monarchy as an ideal is particularly associated with 17th- and 18th-century Europe. In an absolute monarchy, the sovereign wields the ultimate power within the state, and the authority of the sovereign is unlimited by a constitution. The absolute monarch seeks to limit or deny the power of other bodies within the realm, such as the nobility, the Church and parliamentary assemblies.

Absolute monarchs believed they had a God-given dispensation to rule, and this was expressed in the idea of 'the divine right of kings'. This was famously articulated by King James I of England when he addressed Parliament in 1610: 'The state of monarchy is the supremest thing upon earth; for kings are not only God's lieutenants upon earth, and sit upon God's throne, but even by God are called gods.'

James's claims, perpetuated by his stubborn son Charles I, ignored the reality of parliamentary power, ultimately leading to the English Civil War and the execution of the king himself – for treason against his own people. The chaos that reigned during the war encouraged the philosopher Thomas Hobbes to the position that only a monarch with truly absolute power could maintain the safety of his people (see page 212), but this proved unappealing in Britain.

The archetype of the absolute monarch in Europe was Louis XIV of France, who famously declared, *'L'état, c'est moi'* – 'I am the state'. During his long reign (1643–1715), Louis succeeded in weakening the power of the nobility and in concentrating a great deal of power in his own person. Other European monarchs attempted to emulate Louis' achievements, but with limited success. During the 18th and 19th centuries, economic changes – particularly in international trade and in industrialization – brought about a shift in power towards the urban bourgeoisie, who pressed for constitutional government in which they would be represented.

Totalitarianism

Totalitarian regimes not only seek to wield absolute power, but also to control every aspect of life within the state, so that every action and every thought of every citizen accords with their ideology. Totalitarianism is particularly associated with the fascist, Nazi and communist dictatorships of the 20th century, such as Hitler's Germany and Stalin's Soviet Union.

It is unlikely that totalitarianism could have arisen before the development of mass media such as newspapers, radio and cinema, which are used to indoctrinate the populace with endless streams of propaganda. Schools and universities are diverted to similar ends, and the individual's sense of only having significance in the context of the state or the ruling ideology is reinforced by mass rallies. Only institutions sanctioned by the state are permitted – there can be no such thing as civil society (see page 214). Totalitarianism is thus at the other end of the political spectrum to liberal democracy.

Democracy

Democracy literally means 'rule by the people'. It can take the form of direct rule by the citizens of a state, who vote on all issues. Alternatively – and much more commonly – it entails government by the people's elected representatives. Even in representative democracies, some very important issues – such as constitutional changes – are put to the popular vote in referendums.

Democracy first emerged in Greece in the late 6th century BC. In the city-state of Athens, for example, decisions were made by assemblies of all adult male citizens (women and slaves were excluded). In Rome under the Republic (509–27 BC), a form of democratic rule also developed: initially only the noble patrician class was represented (in the Senate), but later the common people, or plebeians, acquired a voice through elected tribunes.

Under the emperors who succeeded the Roman Republic, any pretence of democracy disappeared, and in medieval Europe, although monarchs would sometimes summon parliaments, such assemblies represented only a very narrow section of the population and had little real power.

Democracy in its modern form emerged only slowly. In Britain, for example, the 17th century witnessed a protracted struggle between king and Parliament, with the latter emerging in a dominant position. However, at that stage Parliament, although elected, represented only a tiny portion of the population – the nobility, the Church, the land-owning gentry and some wealthy townsmen (no women had the vote). It was not until the early decades of the 20th century, after a long period of campaigning and agitation, that all British adults – of both sexes – acquired the right to vote.

Similar struggles occurred in other countries to achieve the vote for working people, ethnic minorities and women. Today, most states are – notionally at least – democracies, although in many places elections are rigged by corruption, intimidation, manipulation of the media and the banning of opposition parties.

Voting systems

A variety of different voting systems are employed around the world. In the US presidential elections, each state votes for representatives to an electoral college, which then elects a president. In Britain and various other countries, there is a first-past-the-post system, in which candidates stand for a particular constituency, and the candidate with the most votes in each constituency is returned to Parliament; the party with the most elected members forms the government. The objection to both of these systems is that it is possible for a president or government to be returned with only a minority of the overall vote.

Other countries use the voting system known as proportional representation, under which seats are awarded to each party in proportion to the overall percentage of votes they receive nationally. This gives many smaller parties the opportunity to obtain seats, and makes it less likely that any one party has an overall majority, often leading to coalition governments.

Federalism vs centralism

In some nations, political power is the monopoly of a strong central government, which directly controls the administration of the country right down to local level. Such nations are known as unitary states.

In other countries, the central government may only look after such things as defence and foreign policy, with most internal powers being wielded by the country's constituent states, each of which has its own elected government with powers to pass laws and raise taxes. Such countries are described as federations and have often originated in a voluntary union.

Examples of federations include the USA, Germany, Australia and Canada, while examples of unitary states include France and Britain. Unitary states sometimes devolve power to regional assemblies – such as those formed for Scotland, Wales and Northern Ireland at the end of the 20th century

– but this top-down approach is not the same as a voluntary union created from below.

The most notable example of such a voluntary union is the United States of America, which was established in 1776 when the 13 colonies declared their independence from Britain. After independence was secured, the former colonies were reluctant to surrender any powers to a central government, not wishing to exchange one tyranny for another. Thus when the US Constitution was ratified in 1788 it reserved to the states all powers not specifically assigned to the new federal government. The issue of 'states' rights' – especially the right to decide whether to permit slavery – ultimately led a number of slave-holding states to secede. This resulted in the American Civil War of 1861–5, which was fought by the federal government not primarily to abolish slavery, but to preserve the Union.

In other federations, tensions arise when constituent states dominated by one ethnic or language group – such as the Quebecois in Canada or the Basques in Spain – believe that their interests would be better served by full independence.

Collectivism vs individualism

Collectivism denotes a belief that the rights and interests of the group – such as society or the state – take priority. In contrast, proponents of individualism emphasize the rights and liberties of the citizen as an independent entity. The most extreme manifestation of collectivism is the totalitarian state (see page 226), while the values of individualism are most forcibly expressed by libertarians, of both left and right (see page 254).

In between these two extremes, most political positions have a balance of collectivist and individualist values, suggesting that the citizen has both rights and obligations. Social democrats believe that the state has a big role to play in social provision and the economy, while emphasizing the importance of democratic freedoms. Conservatives see a smaller role for the state, and believe that individuals should be left alone to look after themselves. However, they also value social order and believe in obedience to legal, moral and religious authority.

Utopianism

Utopianism is the belief that it is possible to create a perfect society. It takes its name from *Utopia*, a speculative political essay published in 1516 by the English humanist and statesman Sir Thomas More (1478–1535). In this work, More describes a fictional island called Utopia (from the Greek for 'nowhere land'), supposedly just discovered in the middle of the Atlantic. In this ideal state, everybody cooperates with each other, and both men and women work in the fields and at a specific trade. Education is provided to all, and all possessions are held in common. More is in effect describing an early form of communism (see page 258).

More's work gave its name to a whole genre of literature, including Plato's *Republic* (4th century BC), Sir Francis Bacon's *New Atlantis* (1624) and William Morris's *News from Nowhere* (1890). This genre also includes satirical works, such as Jonathan Swift's *Gulliver's Travels* (1726), and evocations of futuristic anti-utopias ('dystopias'), such as Aldous Huxley's

Brave New World (1932) and George Orwell's *Nineteen Eighty-Four* (1949) – a savage denunciation of Soviet totalitarianism.

In the political sphere, the term utopianism carries the suggestion of impossibility. Thus communism, socialism and anarchism have all been condemned by those further to the right as the products of woolly-headed wishful thinking that ignore the darker side of human nature.

Critics suggest that attempts to create 'perfect' societies inevitably involve what they condemn as 'social engineering' – the most extreme examples of which include forcible collectivization in the Soviet Union under Stalin and the Cultural Revolution in China under Mao, both of which entailed enormous suffering.

On a smaller scale, there have been many attempts to set up utopian communities, involving economic cooperation and communal living. These have ranged from the Dutch Mennonite colony established in Delaware in 1663 and Robert Owen's New Lanark in Scotland in the early years of the 19th century, to Israeli kibbutzim and hippy communes in the 20th century.

Left, right and centre

The imagery of left, right and centre in politics derives from the time of the French Revolution in 1789. In the pre-Revolutionary Estates-General (representative assembly), the aristocracy sat to the right of the king, and the commoners to his left. In the post-Revolutionary National Assembly, the more radical politicians sat on the left, and this seating arrangement became common in other European assemblies.

In modern politics, one might list the following positions from far left to far right: Trotskyites and Maoists; communists; socialists; social democrats (centre-left parties such as the British Labour Party); liberals (centre); conservatives and Christian democrats (and other centre-right parties); fascists (including Nazis and racist-nationalists). At both extremes, parties tend towards totalitarianism (see page 226), while those near the centre are broadly democratic. Some groupings – such as Greens (see page 270) and libertarians (see page 254) – are found at various positions on this spectrum.

Conservatism

In politics, conservatism is a position of the centre-right, and is espoused by such groups as the British Conservative Party, various Christian Democratic parties in Europe, and the Republican Party in the USA. There are two strands to conservatism: 'social conservatives' oppose 'socially liberal' positions on (for example) abortion and gay marriage; while 'fiscal conservatives' believe in small government and low taxation. Many conservatives adhere to both positions.

Conservatives generally respect traditional authority (see page 280) – whether that of the monarch or president, the law, the Church or the father as head of the family. Such institutions are regarded as preservers of social order, without which the worst side of human nature (see page 20) would be given free reign.

Implicit in this is a respect for hierarchy (see page 278): people are born with different capacities and their position in society reflects this. Most modern conservatives are reluctant to defend hereditary privilege, and emphasize that social mobility is possible for those who have both the capacity and the will to improve themselves.

Above all, conservatives believe in private property (see page 306), and that people should have the right to do what they wish with property that they have inherited or earned. There may be a range of positions on this. Some traditional conservatives believe in the importance of the nation as a community, in which the better-off have obligations towards the less fortunate, and that these obligations are best realized by some degree of state support in areas such as health and education, funded by taxation.

But there are also many 'economic liberals' (not to be confused with political or social liberals, see page 252), who believe that the best route to economic prosperity is to let the free market operate without government intervention, either in the form of regulation or taxation. Economic liberalism has become a strong force within many centre-right parties since the 1970s.

Social Darwinism

Social Darwinism comprises a series of political, economic and social beliefs derived from Charles Darwin's theory of evolution by natural selection (see page 196). It originated with the English autodidact Herbert Spencer (1820–1903), who summarized Darwin's theory as 'the survival of the fittest' and argued that this justified unrestrained free-market capitalism, in which competition is valued over cooperation. Spencer was, however, perpetrating an egregious example of the naturalistic fallacy, assuming that 'is' is the same as 'ought' (see page 122).

Social Darwinism gave rise to eugenics, a now-discredited pseudo-science that maintained the poor and underprivileged were of 'inferior stock', and should be prevented from breeding in order to maintain the fitness of the population. Eugenicists also believed that behavioral traits such as a tendency to criminality could be expressed in physiology. 'Scientific' racists seized on such ideas, extending the notion to peoples they regarded as 'inferior' to themselves (see pages 246–9).

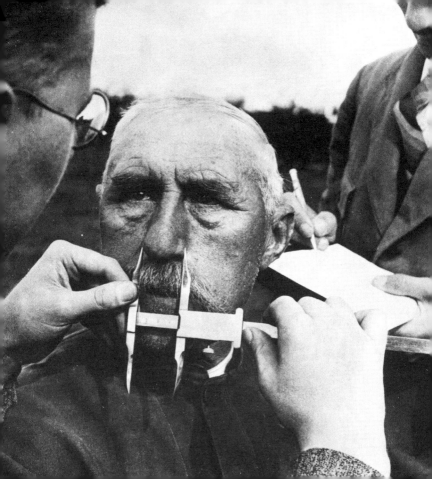

Nationalism

Nationalism is a political ideology that emphasizes the primacy of national identity, based on such factors as ethnicity, language and cultural tradition. The arts have often played an important role in nationalism, and its core appeal has always been more emotional than rational. The nation is held up as a quasi-sacred entity, greater than the sum of the individuals within it.

Nationalist movements have emerged in countries that are agitating for independence from foreign rule, and such liberation struggles may represent a broad political spectrum. Such was the case in 19th-century Europe, the birthplace of modern nationalism. At the start of the century, Germany and Italy consisted of numerous small states, while the nationalities of central Europe were subsumed under the Austrian empire.

The emperors, kings and princes who ruled these territories were by and large absolute monarchs (see page 234), and the opposition to their rule included liberal and democratic as well as nationalist elements. They were swept along by the poets and musicians of the Romantic movement (see page 386), who drew heavily on folk tales and folk music to help forge a new sense of national identity.

After a century of struggle, the rights of the smaller nations of Europe to national self-determination were recognized by the peace settlement that followed the First World War. This in turn encouraged independence movements in the overseas empires of the European powers. Nationalist agitation was sometimes violently resisted by imperial forces, but in the period 1945–75 around a hundred former colonies became independent sovereign states.

Nationalism has its darker side. The nationalist parties that have emerged in established nation-states have tended to stress – sometimes belligerently – the superiority of the nation concerned compared to other peoples and nations. In its more extreme forms, nationalism merges with racism (see page 248) and fascism (see page 250).

Colonialism and imperialism

From the 16th century onwards, a number of European powers competed with each other to establish colonies in distant parts of the world – largely in order to control the profitable trade in raw materials and to provide new markets for their manufactured goods. By the 19th century, inspired by a mixture of religion and racism, colonialists had developed an 'imperial' ethos, with the high moral purpose of bringing what they saw as the advantages of Western civilization to their 'primitive' colonial subjects. Beneath this veneer, however, commercial interests still played a crucial role.

Exposure to Western values of democracy and equality led the educated elites in the colonized countries to question the right of the imperial powers to 'lord it' over them. This gave rise to nationalist movements (see page 245) and a slow and sometimes violent process of decolonization in the second half of the 20th century. Some believe, however, that political imperialism has merely been replaced by economic imperialism.

This famous cartoon of 1892 depicts British imperialist Cecil Rhodes as a colossus striding across Africa.

Racism

Racism is the belief that certain 'races' are not only different from, but also superior to, other 'races'. This may result in discriminatory practices ranging from insulting behaviour and unequal treatment to enforced segregation and even genocide. Such beliefs and practices are now generally condemned on both moral and scientific grounds, but were widespread up to – and beyond – the Second World War.

The concept of 'race' itself is both complex and questionable. In the past, limitations on communications and transport made communities suspicious of outsiders, but this was largely on grounds of language and custom – what we would now call ethnicity. If the outsider adopted the ways of the community, he or she might well find themselves accepted. In this version of race, there is nothing innate about difference.

In the 19th century, there arose a new attitude of superiority towards non-European colonial peoples. This was reinforced by the emergence of various pseudo-scientific theories of race, in which humans around the world were classified into different 'subspecies' according to physical characteristics such as skin colour and physiognomy (differences that modern geneticists discount as very superficial). According to these pseudo-scientific theories, white Europeans were supposedly the most 'evolved' or 'advanced' humans, both physically and mentally.

These theories were taken up by Social Darwinists – proponents of 'the survival of the fittest' in human affairs (see page 242) – and eugenicists, who urged that the breeding of people considered 'inferior' on either intellectual, physical or racial grounds should be restricted, so as not to dilute the quality of the 'stock'. In the earlier 20th century eugenics was considered quite respectable, but it fell out of favour once it became forever associated with the Nazis. Hitler's regime took racism to its ultimate conclusion, exterminating as many as 14 million people – Jews, Slavs, Gypsies and others – whom they regarded as 'subhuman'. It was the largest – though not the last – genocide in history.

Fascism

The carnage of the First World War brought about a bitter mood of disillusion with democratic politics, while the Bolshevik Revolution in Russia in 1917 inspired a widespread fear of communism. It was these circumstances that gave birth in the 1920s and 1930s to fascism in Italy and a number of other countries, including Japan, Spain and Germany.

Fascism is an extreme right-wing form of nationalism (see page 244), with a strongly authoritarian or even totalitarian flavour (see page 226). It varies between countries, but in general fascist movements share a cult of the all-powerful leader, and a dislike of foreigners, ethnic minorities, socialists, communists, liberals and democrats. Its enthusiasm for militarism and territorial expansion contributed to the outbreak of the Second World War. Today, fascism survives in a variety of manifestations, from uniformed skinhead thugs in Russia to far-right anti-immigrant parties in Britain and France that appear content to engage in democratic politics.

The word 'fascism' derives from *fasces*, the ceremonial bundles of sticks around an axe carried by magistrates in ancient Rome.

Liberalism

The word 'liberal' – deriving from the Latin word for freedom – has a variety of shades of meaning, but in general liberals believe in democracy, equality, the rights of the individual and limited government. Some liberals place greater emphasis on tolerance in the social sphere – for example, on matters such as gay rights – while others put the emphasis more on liberty in the economic sphere, upholding free markets and rejecting government regulation, in the same way that many conservatives do.

In the United States, political opinion is conventionally divided between 'conservatives' on the right and 'liberals' on the left. US liberals (many of them associated with the Democratic Party) are secular in outlook, support the rights of minorities and believe in the use of government power to help the underprivileged. In many other countries liberals (such as the British Liberal Democrats), though espousing similar values, are in the centre of politics, with conservatives to the right of them and social democrats and socialists to the left.

Modern liberalism owes its origins to the English philosopher John Locke, who in the late 17th century developed his version of the social contract (see page 212). Locke had a profound influence on some of the Founding Fathers of the USA, notably Thomas Jefferson, who drafted the Declaration of Independence.

The classic exposition of liberalism is *On Liberty* (1859) by the English philosopher John Stuart Mill. In this, Mill argued that individual liberty should only be curtailed where it harms another individual.

More recently the American philosopher John Rawls, in his *Theory of Justice* (1971), outlined an influential redistributive version of liberalism in which he argued that if we did not know what place we would be born into in society, we would choose a society in which everybody had equal rights, and in which there was a minimum of social and economic inequality.

Libertarianism

Libertarians believe in complete freedom for every individual, untrammelled by government, law, religion or social custom. Libertarians are found on both the right and the left. Those on the right are 'economic' liberals who extend their belief in *laissez-faire* capitalism to social behaviour – everything should be permitted in the name of liberty. Libertarians on the left tend to see the rejection of authority and the breaking of social taboos as revolutionary acts, in which transgression is a necessary step towards transformation.

Many libertarians focus on those forms of behaviour that are abhorrent to social conservatives. Thus they demand, for example, the legalization of all recreational drugs from cannabis to heroin, and of all forms of pornography and consensual sexual practice. Individual responsibility is paramount. Those on the right reject the 'nanny state', in which government intervenes to prevent harm, and believe that social problems should be dealt with by market-style solutions.

Socialism

The term 'socialism' encompasses a range of positions, from the centre-left to the far left of politics. Socialism is a child of the Western Industrial Revolution which, in the later 18th and 19th centuries, created a large urban working class who were both disenfranchised and impoverished, and who looked to collective action – whether through democratic politics, trade-union activity or violent revolution – to achieve social justice.

At the core of socialism is a belief in equality. One aspect of this is internationalism, whereby socialists condemn nationalism, racism and imperialism, and advocate solidarity among working people around the world. Belief in equality also entails a belief that society and the economy should be ordered for the common good and not for the benefit of the privileged and/or the most ruthless. Where conservatives and economic liberals believe that it is down to each individual to improve their own lot, and thus that the government should not interfere in the operation of free markets, socialists believe that the success or failure of individuals is very often the result of chances of birth and environment.

Moderate socialists believe that, in order to even out economic and social inequalities, wealth should be redistributed in some way, largely via taxation. Government has a role in helping the underprivileged – for example, by the provision of free education and health care, pensions, unemployment benefit and other aspects of the welfare state, intended to provide a safety net 'from the cradle to the grave'. This is generally the position of social democratic parties, such as the British Labour Party, who believe in a gradual and democratic transformation of society.

More radical socialists, taking their cue from Karl Marx (see page 260), believe that only violent revolution can right social and economic injustice. They believe that socialism is no more than a step on the way to achieving true communism (see page 258), where class, private property and even the state itself are all things of the past.

Communism

In broad terms, communism denotes any society where all property is held in common. Experiments in small-scale 'primitive' communism have appeared at various times – for example, among certain medieval monastic communities, and among some radical groups around the time the English Civil War in the 17th century.

Modern 'scientific' communism originates in *The Communist Manifesto* (1848), written by Karl Marx and Friedrich Engels (see page 260). They believed the industrial working class would overthrow capitalism and establish a 'dictatorship of the proletariat' – a period of socialism with all property owned by the state. Eventually the state itself would be replaced by perfect communism, based on the principle 'From each according to his ability, to each according to his needs.' The 'communist' states established during the 20th century in the Soviet Union and elsewhere never got past state socialism, with the Communist Party exercising dictatorial power.

Marxism

The German thinkers Karl Marx (1818–83) and Friedrich Engels (1820–95), the founders of modern communism, developed an interpretation of history called dialectical materialism, which holds that social development proceeds through struggles between classes, ultimately driven by changes in the dominant mode of economic production.

In the feudal Middle Ages, according to Marx, the mode of production was primarily agricultural, and power was in the hands of the nobility because they owned the land. With the Industrial Revolution of the 18th and 19th centuries, factories and mines replaced land as the main source of wealth, and the bourgeoisie (the capitalist middle class) replaced the feudal aristocracy as the ruling class. Marx predicted that the next phase would come when the exploited proletariat (the industrial working class) rose up and overthrew capitalism establishing a 'dictatorship of the proletariat'. This in turn would give way to 'perfect' communism (see page 258).

In practice, things did not quite work out like that. Marx had predicted that the revolution would start in Germany, where industrialization was well established and there was a substantial urban proletariat. Russia, in contrast, was still a backward feudal society, only just beginning to industrialize at the beginning of the 20th century. The Russian revolutionary Vladimir Ilych Lenin (1870–1924), however, argued that it was possible for a small core of professional revolutionaries to initiate a successful revolution – and proceeded to do so in 1917.

In China, Mao Zedong (1893–1976) further adapted Marxist orthodoxy by mobilizing the revolutionary potential of the vast peasant population – a strategy that brought eventual communist victory in 1949.

Although Marx's predictions have failed to come about, his mode of social, political and economic analysis continues to be influential among many intellectuals. Marxist approaches have been found useful in a wide range of fields, whether looking, for example, at the material or class basis of cultural phenomena or the alienating effects of modern industrial society.

Syndicalism

Syndicalism is a radical form of anti-state, anti-capitalist trade unionism that first arose in France in the 1890s (*syndicat* is the French word for trade union). It was politically influential in the first half of the 20th century, for example in Spain and the USA, where it was taken up by the Industrial Workers of the World (the 'Wobblies'), and remains important in the labour movements of countries such as France and Spain.

Influenced by anarchist thinkers (see page 264), syndicalists advocate industrial action – such as general strikes – as the means to transform society. Contrary to conventional Marxism, they demand that control of the means of production should be transferred not to the state (which they believe will always be a centre of power and privilege) but to trade unions. They regard unions, as free associations of individuals, to be more fundamentally democratic than representative bodies such as parliaments, and are generally suspicious of socialist intellectuals who participate in conventional democracy.

Anarchism

Anarchy is often used as a synonym for 'chaos', but in political terms, anarchists aim not for chaos, but for the disappearance of the state, allowing people to associate freely with each other for the common good. Although they advocate the abolition of the state and all its institutions, anarchists are not the same as nihilists, who reject all established values and advocate destruction for its own sake. Neither are they necessarily the same as libertarians (see page 259), whose values are more individualist than collectivist.

Anarchists believe that humans are by nature both benign and cooperative. They are only corrupted by government, which both exploits and oppresses them. Anarchists are also anti-capitalist, maintaining that industrial capitalism corrupts and disempowers humans and prevents them from realizing their true potential. Although generally regarded as a left-wing tendency, anarchism also condemns conventional Marxism, rejecting its endorsement of state control (see page 260) as a necessary stage on the route to true communism.

The first person to call himself an anarchist was the French philosopher and socialist, Pierre-Joseph Proudhon (1809–65), who famously declared that 'Property is theft.' Although Proudhon and Marx influenced each other, they later fell out. Proudhon believed in peaceful change rather than violent revolution, and advocated cooperatives or individual worker or peasant ownership, as opposed to private, corporate or state ownership, which all involve some degree of control of individuals by other individuals. In contrast to Proudhon, the Russian anarchist Mikhail Bakunin (1814–76) advocated violent seizure of power, both through mass action and individual acts of terrorism. He too fell out with Marx.

Anarchism has never become a mass political movement, although it has proved influential in syndicalism (see page 262). It has also appealed to groups of young, often middle-class radicals, such as the student protestors of 1968 or the anti-globalization activists of the present day.

Communitarianism

Communitarianism is a relatively recent political philosophy, originating in the USA in the later 20th century. It seeks to find a 'third way' between socialism on the one hand, with its emphasis on the role of the state in ordering society (see page 256), and right-wing libertarianism on the other, which asserts the primacy of the individual while denying the importance to humans of community (see page 254).

Traditional conservatives have always emphasized the importance of community, but for them this means hierarchy, authority, and cultural, moral and even religious uniformity. Communitarians tend to hold ground that has been called the 'radical centre'. They believe that citizens have obligations as well as rights, uphold the virtue of civil society (see page 214) in which citizens are 'stakeholders' and emphasize the value of 'social capital', mutually beneficial connections between social networks. Communitarian ideas have had some influence in the USA and UK, both on the centre-left and the centre-right.

Environmentalism

Environmentalism is a broad movement that arose in reaction to the negative impacts that human activity has had on landscape, wildlife and the natural world in general. It places a value on such things, arguing that they should be conserved as amenities for human recreation, as sources of biodiversity and as goods in themselves. As well as protecting pristine habitats, environmentalists also campaign on issues such as pollution, sustainability and global warming.

Prior to the later 18th century and the emergence of the Romantic movement, wild places such as mountains or virgin forests were disparaged as both hostile and hideous, and of no use unless mined or quarried or felled. The Romantics took a different view, finding in wilderness that heightened state of emotion they called the sublime. Poets such as Wordsworth saw humans as part of nature, not in opposition to it, and even depicted nature as some kind of moral teacher.

The Romantics helped to reorient people's relations to the natural world, but so far as practical action is concerned, the environmental movement can be traced back to the Scottish-born American naturalist, John Muir (1838–1914), who successfully campaigned for the creation of the first national parks and in 1892 founded the Sierra Club, the leading conservation body in the USA. Similar bodies were created elsewhere, such as England's National Trust in 1895.

The Romantic movement's idealization of nature was largely an aesthetic reaction to the Industrial Revolution, which radically transformed both societies and landscapes. Industrialization also gave rise to pollution on an unprecedented scale. Although the first legislation to restrict air pollution was introduced in the UK in 1863, things generally got much worse before they began to get better.

In 1962 Rachel Carson's book *Silent Spring* detailed the damaging effects on the food chain caused by pesticides such as DDT, kick-starting a new wave of intensive environmental campaigning, out of which emerged a number of 'Green' political parties (see page 270).

Green politics

In the 1970s, the environmentalist movement gave rise to 'Green' political parties, who emphasize our moral duty to look after the planet on behalf of future generations. Today they are represented in various national legislatures and have even formed coalition governments with larger parties. Typical Green policies include strict regulation of industry and agriculture, reduction of waste, and support for renewable energy. Greens tend to be left-of-centre, with values including ecology, social justice, grassroots democracy and non-violence.

In the past, various far-right nationalist and fascist movements also encouraged respect for nature. The Nazi ideology of 'blood and soil', for example, conjured up a quasi-mystical relationship of the people with the land. Many wealthy conservatives are also concerned with the conservation of wildlife and habitats. However, they have been criticized as merely protecting their own leisure interests and aesthetic values while ignoring the needs of impoverished local people.

Feminism

Feminism is the belief that women should have equal rights to men. The campaign to achieve this, known as the women's movement, traces its origins to the late 18th century, when the British writer Mary Wollstonecraft published *A Vindication of the Rights of Woman* (1792). At this time, women were very much second-class citizens, regarded as the property of their fathers or husbands, and barred from the professions, from higher education and from voting or holding political office.

To campaign against inequality, women had to organize themselves, and the first women's rights convention was held in the USA, at Seneca Falls, New York, in 1848. Many saw winning the right to vote as the first step, and in the later 19th century women's suffrage associations were formed in a number of countries. Their peaceful methods were eclipsed in the early years of the 20th century by the more militant 'Suffragettes', who broke windows, chained themselves to railings and went on hunger strike in pursuit of 'votes for women'. One by one, countries granted women the franchise: for example, Britain and Germany in 1918, the USA in 1920 and France and Italy in 1945.

A new wave of feminism, the 'women's liberation movement', arose during the 1960s, amid a period of radical social change in many Western countries. Many were inspired by the French philosopher Simone de Beauvoir, who had argued in *The Second Sex* (1949) that 'One is not born a woman; one becomes one' – i.e. 'femininity' is not biologically determined, but rather the result of cultural conditioning. Another important text was Betty Frieden's *The Feminine Mystique* (1963).

The new feminists campaigned for equal pay and for access to family planning and childcare, against discrimination on grounds of gender and against all forms of male exploitation and oppression, from pornography to domestic violence. Success has been mixed, but there has undoubtedly been some shift in male attitudes towards women and a raising of women's aspirations – at least among the Western middle classes.

Multiculturalism

Thanks to processes such as migration and globalization, many societies around the world today are composed of a mixture of ethnic groups. Multiculturalism is the policy of accepting and even promoting a range of different ethnic and religious cultures within a society, rather than attempting to impose a single cultural identity. In opposition to multiculturalism, some argue that if immigrants wish to settle in a society, they should assimilate themselves by adopting the values of the 'host' culture. Only thus, they argue, will social cohesion be maintained, and tension and conflict avoided.

Some countries, such as Great Britain, have adopted a degree of multiculturalism, while others, such as France, encourage assimilation and sometimes even enforce it with legislation – such as banning Muslim women from wearing traditional face coverings. The USA has always seen itself as a 'melting pot' of different immigrant peoples, who tend to express their ethnic identities within the context of an overall American identity.

Benvinguts
Bienvenidos
Benvidos
Ongi etorri
Welcome
أهلاً وسهلاً
Bienvenue
Willkommen
歡迎光臨

Secularism vs theocracy

The word theocracy literally means 'rule of God'. The term denotes a state in which the government is dominated by clergy belonging to one particular religion, and in which religious law is the law of the land. Secularism, in contrast, maintains that no religion should have a privileged position within the state, and that religion is entirely a private matter, which should play no part in public life.

From the very beginnings of civilization, religion has been an instrument of temporal as well as spiritual power. The first kings claimed descent from the gods and maintained their power via an assertion of divine authority, backed up with force. Many later states and empires adopted state religions, which bolstered the position of the rulers without necessarily handing power to the priesthood. In pre-Christian Rome, for example, where the emperor was also *pontifex maximus*, or chief priest, religious ritual was largely a matter of public duty and an expression of loyalty to the state.

The Middle Ages saw a number of disputes in Europe between secular rulers and the Catholic Church in Rome, often over who was to have the final say in such matters as ecclesiastical appointments. Things came to a head during the Reformation, when a number of monarchs – such as Henry VIII of England – broke away from Rome to establish their own state churches with themselves at the head.

Although Britain today has a very low level of regular church attendance, there is still an established church, of which the monarch is head, and there are also many state-subsidized religious schools. Ironically, although the USA has a much higher level of church attendance, there is a constitutional separation between church and state – as there is in France, for example.

In the Muslim world, in contrast, there are several countries that are ruled according to strict Islamic law, while the aim of more radical Islamists is to create a global caliphate, in which Islamic law is universally applied.

Hierarchy

Hierarchy is one of the key values of the traditionalist or conservative right. They tend to uphold monarchy and aristocracy, and the hereditary principle whereby both property and status are passed from one generation to the next. In contrast, economic liberals, also on the right, reject inherited political privileges, but not inherited property.

There is a general belief on the right that humans are by their nature unequal. They are therefore mistrustful of egalitarianism (see page 288), which they regard as inevitably resulting in a levelling down, rather than a levelling up. They may back their position up with arguments drawn from social Darwinism (see page 242), in which 'the survival of the fittest' is seen as the 'natural' model for society. Some also claim that there are innate biological differences between the sexes and between the races in matters such as intelligence and disposition, arguments that have been used to justify policies ranging from discrimination to genocide.

Authority and authoritarianism

Those on the right, apart from a few libertarians (see page 254), place a great value on authority. This, they believe, is the key to maintaining social order, which in turn preserves property rights and allows the free market to operate effectively. Some on the right see the need to balance authority with democratic rights, while others are in favour of authoritarian government – whether by an absolute monarch (see page 224) or a dictator.

It was the French Revolution of 1789, and the disorder that followed, which provoked right-wing thinkers to a defence of traditional authority. The Savoyard philosopher Joseph de Maistre (1754–1821) blamed the bloodbath on the secularist and liberal thinkers of the Enlightenment, and argued for the restoration of absolute monarchy and a return to patriarchal authority in both state and family. In addition, de Maistre believed the Roman Catholic Church should have a privileged position within the state, and argued that Christian morality should be enforced through the law. This kind of theocratic thinking has been welcomed in regimes as diverse as Franco's Spain and the Iran of the ayatollahs.

The influential Anglo-Irish conservative theorist Edmund Burke (1729–97) criticized the French Revolutionaries from a somewhat different perspective. He believed that established authority was the means by which customs and traditions are preserved, and that they in turn are the means by which the accumulated wisdom and experience of humanity is transmitted to future generations. Burke believed that the destruction of authority would lead to extreme permissiveness and chaos, in turn leading to dictatorship.

During the Cold War, Western democracies – particularly the USA – made a distinction between those regimes they considered totalitarian (see page 226), such as the Soviet Union and its allies, and those that were merely authoritarian, such as right-wing military dictatorships. The latter were often supported, regardless of their human rights record, if they were considered useful bulwarks against communism.

Progress

As a concept, progress assumes the possibility that things can, and indeed will, get better. Implicit in this is a benign view of human nature (see page 20) – that we are improvable, given the right circumstances. Progress is both a belief and a value, and is shared by liberal, radical and left-wing parties. In contrast, reactionaries and conservatives take a more pessimistic view, denying the possibility of improvement. Indeed, they often look back to some past 'golden age', claiming that things have since gone to the dogs.

The idea of progress can be traced back to the 16th century, with the emergence of secular humanism and the Scientific Revolution. Since that time, science and technology have made enormous advances, largely for the benefit of humanity. Similarly, few would deny there has been some improvement in the ways we treat each other – for example (in the West at least), through the abolition of child labour and slavery.

Liberty

Liberty, together with its synonym 'freedom', is one of the most overused and abused words in the political lexicon. Demagogues, charlatans, patriots, populists and tyrants have all wrapped themselves in the flag of liberty when it suited them. And few can resist its appeal, when faced with rhetoric such as this, from the Declaration of Arbroath, Scotland's 1320 assertion of independence from the English: 'For it is not for glory, nor riches, nor honour that we fight, but for Freedom only, which no good man lays down but with his life.'

The clarion call of liberty held a particular appeal to the American Revolutionaries. The liberty they envisaged was freedom from interference by the British government in their domestic affairs. This was a very circumscribed vision of liberty, however, given that it allowed for the perpetuation of slavery and failed to give political rights to women.

The sort of freedom that the American Founding Fathers had in mind has been characterized as 'negative' freedom – freedom from government. To this end they included a Bill of Rights in the Constitution, listing the things that government could not do to the individual, such as depriving them of freedom of speech or of religion.

The upholding of negative freedom is a basic platform of political liberalism (see page 252). Further to the right, freedom from government interference in the operation of the market is the fundamental demand of economic liberals.

In contrast, the left uphold 'positive' freedom. The fact that one is not legally prevented from doing something does not necessarily give one the power to do it. Positive freedom involves governments providing the conditions in which people are free to achieve their aims and make the most of their talents – even if this may limit the freedom of some individuals to do what they wish.

Toleration

Toleration of the rights of others to say, think and believe what they wish – a core value of liberalism – has had a chequered history. In medieval Europe, for example, the general tendency was to persecute those who held minority religious beliefs, while even today, those who hold dissident views in totalitarian and authoritarian states are dealt with harshly.

Toleration as a value came to prominence with the 18th-century Enlightenment. 'I may not agree with what you say,' declared Voltaire (1694–1778), one of the leading figures of the movement, 'but I will defend to the death your right to say it.' However, even in modern liberal democracies, constraints may be placed on freedom of speech – in the form, for example, of laws against incitements to violence or racial hatred. The key test in such cases may be whether a statement is likely to lead to physical harm. However, there are considerable debates about whether certain statements should be banned merely because they cause offence.

Equality

The first of the 'self-evident truths' asserted in the American Declaration of Independence of 1776 is that 'All men are created equal.' It is a statement that runs directly counter to the claims of inherited privilege embodied in the British monarchy, from which the Americans were seeking their independence. But what was the nature of this equality? It was not one that embraced either black slaves or women. But it was a start: all free adult males in the new Republic had equal rights, including the right to vote.

The version of equality that became established in the USA was that everybody had the potential to improve themselves, and that accidents of birth should have no effect on one's life chances. Several of America's 19th-century presidents were proud of the fact that they were born in a log cabin. Similarly, a number of leading industrialists of the period also came from humble origins.

Those on the left, however, would say that equality of opportunity only becomes a reality when the state ensures that everybody gets the same start in life – for example, by providing free education, health care and adequate housing. This can only be achieved by some degree of redistribution of wealth via taxation, thus infringing on the property rights of the better-off. Under 'perfect' communism, all private property would be abolished and everybody would enjoy a similar standard of living.

The left is also committed to equal rights regardless of race, religion, gender, sexual orientation and so on, and may attempt to counter discrimination against various minorities through 'affirmative action' – for example, by guaranteeing a certain proportion of government jobs to a particular ethnic group.

The right, meanwhile, criticize affirmative action for discriminating against the better-qualified. They are also critical – to varying degrees – of wealth redistribution, which they see as a levelling down, rather than a levelling up, as well as an infringement of property rights.

Justice

Justice has been one of the most important concepts in moral, legal and political philosophy since the time of the ancient Greeks. In *The Republic* Plato rejects the idea that it merely serves the interests of those in power. Aristotle distinguishes between the sort of justice that awards an individual his or her 'just deserts', in the form of rewards or punishments, and the sort of justice that ensures that goods are equally distributed.

Aristotle's first form is what legal systems aim to administer – although, of course, not all laws may be just. His second is generally called 'social justice', the achievement of which lies very much in the political sphere, and is intimately tied into ideas about equality (see page 288). Implicit in the idea of social justice is that everybody has equal rights, which for those on the left inevitably calls for some degree of redistribution of wealth.

Human rights

Human rights are distinguished from civil rights or civil liberties (see page 296) in that the former are considered 'natural' and universal, whereas the latter – which overlap with the former – are possessed by citizens of a particular state and are protected by law. Human rights also include economic, social and cultural rights, such as the right to employment, health care and education, which governments have a duty to provide.

During the Middle Ages, the theologian St Thomas Aquinas argued that the secular law of the state should be measured against 'natural law', based on Christian principles. In the Enlightenment of the 17th and 18th centuries, philosophers sought to develop ideas of natural law and natural rights based on reason, rather than divine revelation. Such thinking was influential on both the American and French Revolutionaries, and was embodied, for example, in the American Bill of Rights (see page 296).

The idea that human rights should be universal emerged slowly, beginning with the anti-slavery movement in the later 18th century. From the middle of the 19th century, humanitarians became increasingly concerned about the fate of both civilians and combatants in wartime, leading to the Geneva Conventions, a series of international treaties agreed between 1864 and 1949 governing the humane treatment of non-combatants, wounded soldiers and prisoners of war.

In 1948, in the wake of the atrocities of the Second World War, the United Nations issued a Universal Declaration of Human Rights, although the UN has often appeared to have neither the will nor the power to enforce this.

Regional agreements, such as the European Convention on Human Rights drafted in 1950, have proved more effective; in this case, any individual who believes their rights have been violated by a signatory state can take their case to the European Court of Human Rights, which has the power to overturn the judgement of national courts.

Animal rights

To what extent should the rights we accord to humans be extended to animals? Until Darwin's theory of evolution (see page 196), humans and animals were regarded as entirely separate entities, but now we know there is no categorical distinction, the question demands attention.

Although the 19th century saw the introduction of legislation to prevent cruelty to animals, the concept that animals might have rights in the same way as humans only emerged in the later 20th century. At its starkest, the animal rights position can be stated simply: animals have the right not to be treated as property – thus, they should not be used as food, clothing or for research or entertainment. Across what range of species these or other rights should be extended is unclear. For example, are we prepared to grant the right to life to parasitic worms that cause untold human suffering around the world?

Civil liberties

Civil liberties or civil rights constitute a subset of universal human rights (see page 292). They are enjoyed by the citizens of a particular state, and are protected by law – indeed, they often form part of a country's constitution. Civil liberties comprise certain freedoms – such as freedom of expression and freedom to vote – that the government is prohibited from infringing.

In John Locke's version of the social contract (see page 212), outlined in the late 17th century, people consent to exchange their natural rights for civil rights, guaranteed by government. If the government fails to uphold these, the people are free to withdraw their consent to be governed.

Such ideas were influential on both the American and French Revolutions, and in 1791 the Bill of Rights was incorporated into the US Constitution. The rights enumerated therein include freedom of religion, speech, the press, petition and peaceful assembly; the prohibition of trying someone twice for the same offence; the right not to be deprived of life, liberty or property without due process of law; and the right of an accused person to a speedy and public trial before an impartial jury. At the time, these rights of citizenship were not extended to black slaves in America, and even after emancipation, full civil rights for African Americans were not achieved until the great civil rights campaigns of the 1950s and 1960s.

Civil liberties are now taken for granted in Western liberal democracies. However, governments by their nature have a tendency to erode individual freedoms – either because of the nature of bureaucracies, or because they regard the restriction of certain freedoms as necessary to preserve security or enhance the common good. It is up to the organs of civil society – such as the American Civil Liberties Union in the USA or the pressure group Liberty in the UK – to challenge governments, through the courts if necessary.

Exceptionalism

Exceptionalism is the doctrine that one's own people or country has some special status and destiny. This may be thought of as ordained by God or Providence. In the 19th century, for example, British imperialists believed they had a mission to bring 'superior' British values to benighted parts of the world, while today ultra-religious Jews believe that God gave them the Palestinian land they now occupy on the West Bank, in defiance of international law.

The doctrine of exceptionalism is perhaps most pervasive in the USA. It is part of the national mythology that God inspired the early colonists, such as the Pilgrim Fathers, to come to America, and that settlers of European origin had a 'manifest destiny to overspread the continent allotted by Providence'. Many in the USA still believe that their country has a special purpose, to hold up some kind of beacon to the rest of the world.

The Landing of the Pilgrim Fathers in America, by Charles Lucy (1868)

Unilateralism and multilateralism

The terms unilateralism and multilateralism – literally meaning 'one-sidedness' and 'many-sidedness' – were for a long time heard largely in the context of nuclear disarmament. However, they have more recently come to prominence in relation to the way that states conduct their foreign policies.

During the Cold War, the leading powers on both sides assembled huge arsenals of nuclear weapons – more than enough to destroy the world several times over. The theory was that this would act as a deterrent (see page 218) against one side launching a first strike. However, many anti-nuclear campaigners in the West believed that deterrence was both immoral and dangerous. They called for their own side to unilaterally disarm, and hoped that this would persuade the other side to follow suit.

Opponents of the unilateralists thought that the latter were hopelessly naive. They thought that only a multilateral approach

– by which all sides agreed to reduce, or even eliminate, their arsenals – was wise. Over the last few decades, both the USA and the Soviet Union (and its successor, the Russian Federation), have signed a succession of treaties reducing their nuclear stockpiles, while still holding large numbers of weapons.

With tensions eased since the ending of the Cold War in 1990, international concern is now directed at nuclear proliferation, especially at preventing unstable or rogue states or even terrorist organizations acquiring nuclear, chemical or biological weapons of mass destruction.

In terms of the conduct of foreign policy, it was said, for example, that the administration of President George W. Bush took a unilateralist approach, acting without necessarily securing an international consensus. 'You are either with us, or you are with the terrorists,' Bush stated in the wake of 9/11. On coming into office in 2009, President Barack Obama promised to take a more conciliatory, multilateral approach. 'We will extend a hand,' he told America's enemies, 'if you will unclench your fist.'

Economics

Dubbed 'the Dismal Science' by the Scottish historian and political philosopher Thomas Carlyle (1795–1881), economics is the study of commercial activity, analysing how goods and services are produced, distributed, exchanged and consumed. Although various economic theories had been mooted over the previous centuries, modern economics owes its origin to another Scot, Adam Smith (1723–90), whose *The Wealth of Nations* (1776) identified three major factors in production and the wealth of a nation: land, labour and capital.

As a subject, economics is usually divided into microeconomics and macroeconomics. Microeconomics deals with issues facing individuals and firms, while macroeconomics deals with the economy on a national scale and issues such as inflation, unemployment and growth. Some of the key debates in economics concern the degree to which government should attempt to direct and regulate the economy, and such debates form part of the broader sphere of politics.

BID	OFFER	EXECUTE	VOLUME CHANGE	STOCK NAME	STATUS	BID	OFFER	EXECUTE
0.0 1	0.02			SET		16027	3.59	0.36
0.09	0.10	0.02		SET50		12-3 1	3.02	0.44
0.03	0.04	0.09	100.00	SET100		12-3 1	6.08	0.40
0.05	0.06	0.03	80.00	AGRI		12-3 1	0.95	0.40
1.87	0.06	0.03	50.00	BANK		12-3 1	-4.15	-1 1
9	1.89	0.06	50.00	BUILD		12-3 1	6.9 1	
3 1	10	1.87	18.35	COMUN		12-3 1	0.15	
1.4 1	32.75	9.50	18.0 1	FIN		12-3 1	7.3 1	
0.73	1.14	35	13.82	ENERG		12-3 1	407.68	
0.09	0.78	1.43	12.60	FOOD		12-3 1	-2 143	
	0.10	0.73	12.3 1					
0.02		0.10	11.11	INSUR		12-3 1	-2439	
0.02	0.03	0.02	-33.33	PRINT		12-3 1	-5435	
0.03	0.03	0.02	-33.33	PROP		12-3 1	-0.39	
16.10	0.04	0.03	-25.00	TEXT		12-3 1	6.1	
352	17.60	13.50	-20.59	BCP-DR.		18.30	18	
1.8 1	356	354	-14.90	ASIAN		340	3	
16.90	2.30	2.30	-13.53	CPF		23.20	2	
0.94	19	16.90	-11.05	CPI		4.36		
0.09	0.96	0.98	-10.09	GFPT		8.10		
0.22	0.10	0.09	-10.00	LEE		3.24		
	0.23	0.23	-8.00					
0.82	0.0 1	0.0 1	100.00	SSF		6.80		
18.50	13.50	14.58	29.4 1	STA		88.38		
0.05	0.04	0.05	25.00	UPOIC		13		
0.06	0.05	0.06	25.00					

Economic systems

The extent to which governments in different countries become involved in economic affairs largely depends on the political complexion of the government. In most countries the government not only regulates the economy to one degree or another, but also is itself a major player, both as a provider of services (and sometimes also goods) and as a consumer of goods and services provided by the private sector.

The different economic systems that operate in countries around the world can be plotted on a spectrum. At one extreme there is the capitalist free-enterprise economy, in which the means of production is entirely in private ownership, in the form of individuals and firms. The government plays little role in economic decision-making, which is highly decentralized. Prices and production are entirely determined by the laws of supply and demand (see page 310) operating across numerous markets.

At the other extreme is the socialist 'command' economy – a rarity since the collapse of communism in eastern Europe and the demise of the Soviet Union in the period 1989–91. In such economies, production, distribution and consumption are all planned centrally. The state owns all the land and all the industry, and allocates resources to different producers according to a national plan. Similarly, goods are distributed to consumers according to quotas.

In practice, the majority of countries have a 'mixed' economy. In this model, most production – and increasingly most services (such as power and transport) – is in the hands of the private sector, but the government still regulates markets and also adjusts such things as taxes, tariffs, interest rates and the money supply in order to achieve certain key objectives. These objectives may include securing full employment, promoting economic growth and avoiding inflation and deficits in the balance of payments – the balance between the amount a country imports and how much it exports.

Property

Property is anything of value, whether tangible (such as land or buildings) or intangible (such as intellectual property – for example, the copyright on a work of art or the patent on an invention). In law and political theory, property is also the right to own something, and this may embrace the rights to consume, sell, rent, mortgage, transfer, exchange or destroy one's property.

Socialists and communists believe that many things – such as the means of production (land, factories, mines, etc.) – should be in public (state) ownership. In contrast, conservatives and liberals – following the 17th-century English philosopher John Locke – argue that individuals have a natural right to property on which they have expended labour, and that this right is transferable. Furthermore, they maintain that the right to private property is an essential condition of freedom. Without private ownership, they argue, there can be no such thing as individuals, only members of a collective.

Capitalism

Capitalism is the dominant economic system in the world today. It is based on capital, which is wealth that can be used for the production of further wealth, typically by investing it in some business. In a capitalist economy, the principal means of production, distribution and exchange are privately owned, by individuals or companies. Capitalists – individuals who own capital – are free to use their property to generate profit, in open competition with each other.

Capitalism developed at the time of the Industrial Revolution in the 18th and 19th centuries. Prior to that, competition was often restricted – for example, the right to trade or manufacture certain goods was often in the gift of the monarch, and resulted in many inefficient monopolies. This state of affairs was criticized by Adam Smith, whose *The Wealth of Nations* argued that if every individual is free to pursue their own economic self-interest, then the cumulative effect will be to benefit society as a whole.

Following Smith, defenders of capitalism argue that it is the most efficient economic system, as competition forces producers to keep prices low and quality high, thus benefiting consumers. They also argue that it is only just for capitalists to be highly rewarded, since they put their wealth at risk when investing in a business.

Critics claim that workers within a capitalist system are just as exposed to risk as the capitalist, since they will lose their livelihood if the company they work for goes bust. Critics also suggest that the logical aim of a company in a capitalist system is to compete so successfully that it puts its rivals out of business, and therefore achieves a monopoly, charging what it likes for its products and neglecting quality. To counter this, many countries have laws to prevent the creation of monopolies – and indeed many other laws to limit economic freedom for the good of society as a whole.

Supply and demand

In *The Wealth of Nations*, Adam Smith explained how numerous individuals acting in their own economic self-interest unwittingly benefit society as a whole. He called this the operation of 'an invisible hand', by which he meant the laws of supply and demand, two of the most fundamental concepts in economics.

Demand is the quantity of a product (goods or services) that consumers are able or willing to purchase. Supply is the quantity of a product that producers are able or willing to sell. Demand and supply vary with price. The higher the price, the less consumers are willing or able to buy, but the more producers want to sell, to maximize their profits. The lower the price, the more consumers are willing or able to buy, but the less producers want to sell, as their profit is eroded. In free markets, the price at which demand matches supply at any one time is called the equilibrium price.

The market

At the heart of capitalist economies is the market – the arena in which goods, services and resources are bought and sold. Markets operate through the laws of supply and demand (see page 310), and require competition to work. They are therefore distinct from mere trading, which needs no more than two people; a market requires at least three participants, so that there is competition on at least one side.

Markets range in scale from local farmers' markets, with perhaps a dozen stalls, through a town high street or shopping mall, where a range of retail outlets selling similar goods compete with each other, to international commodity or currency markets that operate in the virtual world of global computer networks. There are also labour markets: for example, some governments seek to encourage foreign investors to build factories in their countries by affording workers less legal protection and fewer rights than competitor countries.

Believers in unfettered free markets maintain that they are the most efficient way to run an economy. Firms that cannot supply goods and services of sufficient quality and at a price that consumers demand simply go to the wall, while their more efficient competitors thrive. This, free-marketeers assert, benefits both producers (who make a profit) and consumers (who get what they want at the price they are prepared to pay).

Critics point out that there are limits to the effectiveness of free markets. For example, the laws of supply and demand do not necessarily meet social needs such as transport services in remote areas, nor do they constrain producers from polluting the environment – and neither do they prevent the concentration of wealth in the hands of a small number of individuals. In these and other instances, societies often agree to the need for some degree of government intervention, in the form of subsidies, regulation and taxation.

Labour

Labour denotes both the workforce as a whole, especially wage-earning employees, and any paid-for service supplied by workers in the production of wealth. In totally unregulated labour markets, according to the laws of supply and demand (see page 310), workers must compete against each other by offering to work more for less pay. To counter this, workers form trade unions, which engage in collective bargaining with employers in an attempt to ensure equal pay for equal work.

The English economist David Ricardo (1772–1823) developed what is known as the 'labour theory of value'. This holds that the exchange-value of a good or service is determined solely by the amount of labour involved in its production. Karl Marx (see page 260) developed this idea, arguing that the capitalist pays his workers less than the value their labour has added to the goods, and that the 'surplus labour' he obtains for free creates 'surplus value' – the capitalist's profit.

Free trade vs protectionism

Free trade is the policy of allowing trade between nations without any restriction. Barriers to free trade may take the form of quotas (physically limiting the volume of imports), tariffs (taxes or duties on imports and exports), exchange controls (limitations made by central banks on the amount of foreign currency made available to purchase imports) or subsidies to domestic producers. All of these restrictive measures amount to what is called 'protectionism' – the policy of shielding one's own economy from the full effects of international competition.

Protectionism was almost universal in one form or another until Adam Smith argued in *The Wealth of Nations* that if one country was rich in a particular resource, or particularly good at making some product, it made for greater efficiency and thus contributed to greater overall wealth if that country was allowed to export freely to other countries.

The advocates of free trade who followed Smith in the 19th century argued that protectionism often benefited only a small number of producers, at the expense of the rest of the population. In particular, they pointed to Britain's Corn Laws, which limited imports of grain to keep the domestic price high for the benefit of British farmers. However, this meant that British workers had to pay high prices for bread, and manufacturers complained that in consequence there was little surplus income to purchase their products.

Although the Corn Laws were repealed in 1846, protectionist measures continued to be the norm in international trade – particularly during economic downturns. In the second half of the 20th century, a number of transnational free-trade areas and common markets were created, but these still created trade barriers to non-members. The World Trade Organization holds regular rounds of talks to try to extend free trade internationally. Some argue, however, that unrestricted free trade has a tendency to benefit wealthy nations at the expense of the economic development of poorer countries.

Keynesianism

Keynesianism is the economic doctrine developed by the English economist John Maynard Keynes (1883–1946) in the wake of the mass unemployment of the Great Depression of the 1930s. While other economists argued that free markets would soon create full employment if workers accepted lower wages, Keynes believed that high unemployment was the result of inadequate overall demand for goods and services, and that cutting workers' wages only reduced demand further.

In order to stimulate demand, Keynes advocated government intervention – for example, through funding of public works. The USA pursued these policies in the 1930s under President F.D. Roosevelt's New Deal, resulting in huge projects such as the Hoover Dam (opposite). By the 1950s and 1960s Keynesianism was adopted by many Western governments. In the 1970s Keynes's ideas came under attack by monetarists (see page 322), but they are still widely influential and proved effective in the aftermath of the financial crisis of 2007–8.

Growth

In economic terms, growth is the increase in overall production of goods and services in an economy, over a specified period of time. Governments make growth one of the key targets of their policies, as it contributes to the prosperity of the community, allowing consumers to purchase more, and also enabling government to provide better services, such as education and health. All this results in an increase in the standard of living of a population.

A number of factors can influence a nation's economic growth: increases in the quantity and quality of its capital goods (such as industrial machinery), of the labour force and of natural resources; increases in the efficient use of these factors, leading to higher productivity; technological advances and product innovation; and increases in overall demand. More efficient production and distribution makes for cheaper goods and may also lead to increases in the real pay of workers, which in turn stimulates demand.

All these factors are typically at play when a country industrializes – a process that happened in Europe and North America during the Industrial Revolution of the 18th and 19th centuries, and is happening today in countries such as Brazil, India and China, where growth rates currently far outstrip those in the West.

Making growth a core aim has been criticized from a number of perspectives. Growth may result in the creation of artificial demand, by which consumers are persuaded that it is essential for them to have the latest product, even though they hitherto had no inkling of such a need.

Unlimited growth may also result in the depletion of unrenewable natural resources, such as metals and fossil fuels. It may also be accompanied by industrial and agricultural practices that do lasting damage to the environment. Some argue therefore that growth should be limited to levels that are sustainable for the planet in the long term.

Monetarism

Monetarism is an economic doctrine that has been influential since the 1970s, and is closely associated with US economist Milton Friedman (1912–2006). Monetarism holds that the key factor in the economy is the money supply – the total amount of money in an economy, in the form of coin, currency and bank deposits. If the money supply is increased without being balanced by an increase in the production of goods and services, demand will increase, resulting in inflation.

In opposition to Keynesianism (see page 318), monetarists maintain that, apart from managing the money supply, governments should not intervene in the economy. Along with a belief in the free market (see page 312), they also reject the aim of full employment, arguing that a certain level of unemployment helps to keep wages down and control inflation. In the wake of high inflation in the 1970s, monetarism was adopted by several governments in the 1980s, such as those of President Reagan in the USA and Mrs Thatcher in the UK.

Development

In the economic sphere, the term 'development' denotes the process by which poorer societies based on subsistence agriculture transform into modern industrialized economies. Although sometimes taken to be the equivalent of economic growth (see page 320), development usually implies structural transformation, and therefore the changes involved are qualitative as well as quantitative.

Development has been an international issue since the end of the Second World War, when the era of European colonialism began to come to an end (see page 246). Although the balance of political power shifted, the developed world – keen to maintain overseas markets for its manufactured goods and to ensure a steady supply of natural resources and agricultural commodities – still dominated the former colonies economically. Aid was often tied to the economic interests of the donor country – and, especially during the Cold War, tied to its political interests as well. For many years, one-fifth of the world consisted of rich nations, while four-fifths remained poor.

After the Cold War, the picture began to change. Countries such as China abandoned socialist command economies and began a process of rapid economic growth. Today one-fifth of the world's economies remain rich, three-fifths are emerging, industrializing and catching up rapidly, and one-fifth (mainly in sub-Saharan Africa) remain poor. Various factors have been identified that hinder development in such countries, including civil war, poor leadership, corruption and over-reliance on a single natural resource such as oil or diamonds.

In 2001, the United Nations agreed eight 'Millennium Development Goals'. These seek to achieve: the eradication of hunger and extreme poverty; universal primary education; gender equality and the empowerment of women; a reduction in child mortality; improvement in maternal health; effective measures against HIV/AIDS, malaria and other diseases; environmental sustainability; and a Global Partnership for Development. It was intended that all these should be achieved by 2015, but progress has proved slow.

Globalization

Globalization began with the European voyages of discovery of the 15th and 16th centuries, which ushered in a new era of international trade, migration and cultural exchange. The process has accelerated in recent decades, particularly since the end of the Cold War. Political and trade barriers have tumbled, and many Western companies have moved their manufacturing bases to developing countries where wages are lower. Revolutions in transport and communications – such as containerization and the Internet – have also played their part.

Globalization has resulted in considerable economic growth in 'emerging' economies, such as India and China, and also contributes to the spread of Western democratic values. However, critics point out that it has increased inequalities and the exploitation of workers in the developing world, that local producers are elbowed aside by vast multinational companies, and that cultural diversity is threatened by bland homogeneity, in everything from fast food to films and fashion.

Game theory

We tend to think of economics as consisting of equations and graphs, but it is an inexact science that also has to take into account the ways that humans behave – ways that are not always rational. One of the tools that economists use is game theory, which also has applications in other fields.

Game theory is a branch of applied mathematics, but involves a very different approach to the applied mathematics used in the physical sciences, where what is required is a way of predicting what will happen in the non-human world.

The field was originated by two Americans, John von Neumann and Oskar Morgenstern, in their book *The Theory of Games and Economic Behaviour* (1944). In this, they compared economics to a game in which the players seek to anticipate each other's moves. Game theory has since been deployed in many fields where the decisions made by the participants affect the outcome, from military strategy to politics to evolutionary biology. Game theory goes beyond classical probability theory, in that it also takes into account the psychology of factors such as self-interest, bargaining and bluffing.

One of the most famous scenarios in game theory is the so-called 'prisoner's dilemma'. In this, two people accused of committing a crime together are interviewed separately. Each one is given the same options: to confess, or to remain silent. They are informed that if one confesses, and the other stays silent, the confessor will be freed, while the other will be sentenced to ten years. If both stay silent, each will receive a one-year sentence. If both confess, each will get five years.

Mathematically, the optimum choice is for both to stay silent. However, game theory suggests that such is human selfishness that both will confess, in the hope of being acquitted, rather than running the risk of being the only one to stay silent, and so receiving the maximum sentence. The optimum choice is therefore not the obvious one – although if the dilemma is repeated again and again, then the participants can learn to cooperate.

Sociology

Sociology is the study of human societies, particularly their development, organization, functioning and classification. The term was coined in the 19th century by the French positivist philosopher Auguste Comte (see page 66), who believed that sociology could become one of the sciences. The discipline was later developed by fellow Frenchman Emile Durkheim (1858–1917) and the German Max Weber (1864–1920).

Today, because the findings of sociology cannot be tested experimentally, it is regarded as a 'social science', alongside fields such as social anthropology, politics, economics and psychology. Methods used include statistical surveys of attitudes, behaviour and social conditions, participant observation, and systematic comparisons of different societies. Fields of interest include social stratifications (such as class), crime and deviance, and the ways that the structure of society as a whole and institutions as diverse as schools or the military influence individual and collective behaviour.

Anthropology

Anthropology literally means 'the study of humans', and as such is very broad in scope, taking in archaeology and linguistics as well as physical and social (or cultural) anthropology. It may thus combine elements from the physical sciences and the humanities as well as the social sciences. When modern anthropology first emerged in the 19th century, all these subjects were studied together, but today the different branches of anthropology are regarded in many universities as entirely separate, and are studied in different departments, or even faculties.

Physical anthropology – the study of the origins, evolution and physical diversity of human beings – is now regarded as a branch of human biology. It may draw on archaeology, genetics and ethology (the study of animal behaviour), as well as looking at the interaction of human biology with the environment and with culture and society – the things that distinguish humans from other animals. Some of the earlier work of physical anthropologists in comparing human 'races' via techniques such as skull measurement has now been discredited, tainted as it has become by pseudo-scientific racism (see page 248).

Social anthropology is concerned with the cultural and social constructs of human groups. When the discipline developed in the 19th and earlier 20th centuries, the focus tended to be on 'primitive', pre-industrial societies, although over recent decades anthropologists have adapted their approach to look at modern industrial societies as well.

The systematic comparison of different cultures is known as ethnology, while ethnography is the study of a particular culture or society. Ethnography is typically undertaken by participant-observation, and the anthropologist may immerse him- or herself in the culture concerned for lengthy periods. Among the many topics of interest to social anthropologists – both from an ethnographic and a more theoretical point of view – are kinship, gender relations, childrearing, customs and rituals, myth and religion, consumption and exchange, games and festivals, and the products of material culture such as tools, food and costume.

Relativism

The concept of relativism has a particular importance in anthropology, where it is common to distinguish cultural, moral, cognitive and methodological relativism. Cultural relativism – the idea that no culture is 'superior' to any other – originated in the Enlightenment, but was only established as a principle of anthropology in the early 20th century, with the aim of replacing ethnocentric approaches with a new objectivity.

Cultural relativism led some anthropologists to adopt a moral relativism that denied, for example, universal human rights (see page 292). Others proposed a cognitive relativism, maintaining that different cultures exist in different spheres of thought and knowledge, and that it is difficult or impossible to cross the boundaries between them. Moral and cognitive relativism are both now largely discredited, but anthropologists still pursue methodological relativism, by which they aim to suspend their own cultural or moral prejudices while attempting to understand the beliefs and behaviours of others.

Extreme body modification such as that seen among the Burmese Kayan Lahwi or 'Giraffe-Neck Women' is a typical example of a cultural phenomenon that seems strange by Western standards.

Ritual

Rituals are of particular interest to anthropologists, who seek to understand the significance of actions that to outsiders appear random but which to the participants may be of great importance – or totally routine. Rituals are often associated with the practice of a religion, but the term can embrace any formal actions that are prescribed by the traditions of the community concerned. These actions may be primarily symbolic, but some may also have a strong functional component.

Examples of rituals range from rites of passage (such as weddings and funerals) and acts of worship (such as making an offering) to initiations (such as joining a club) and collective expressions of respect or approbation (such as curtain calls at the end of a theatrical production) – to name but a few.

Sometimes special places are set aside for the performance of rituals, particularly those that involve many people. Examples include temples, theatres and sports arenas. Some rituals may be performed anywhere – for example, in many societies two people when they meet shake hands or embrace or kiss each other.

The purposes of rituals vary: religious rituals often fulfil emotional and spiritual needs, and may also help to reinforce social bonds and express shared beliefs and values – as do many other collective rituals. Some rituals mark important transitions – rites of passage recognize a change of status, whether it be circumcision when a boy reaches puberty or a wake to mark a death.

Anthropologists have sought to find underlying structures in rituals, to see whether the rituals of different cultures embody universal elements in human behaviour. For example, it has been pointed out that all rites of passage incorporate three phases: separation, transition and incorporation. These three phases occur in all sorts of ceremonies, from the process by which Masai boys in east Africa become warriors, to the Scottish custom of first-footing at Hogmanay.

Myth

Human societies have universally created myths both as a means of explaining the world and as a way of reinforcing their own group identity. Myths may seek to account for natural phenomena – from the seasons to the origins of humanity – and also such things as evil, death, taboos and time. Myths that recount the creation of the universe are known as cosmogonies and are common to all pre-scientific peoples. Although science has usurped the explanatory role of such myths, their emotional and spiritual resonance may survive.

The role of myth in unifying communities – from tribes to nations – continues to be important. Such myths often involve national heroes (such as Joan of Arc or George Washington) or historical events (such as the landing of the *Mayflower* or the evacuation at Dunkirk). The process of myth-making (known as mythopoeia) is an ongoing one – but one that is increasingly in the hands of government propagandists and public-relations experts.

Class

Today, we think of social stratifications and divisions primarily in terms of class. However, there are a number of different ways in which societies can be structured. There are, for example, vertical divisions, such as those based on gender, ethnicity, religion or language, and these, even today, cut across horizontal divisions such as class.

Horizontal divisions or stratifications have been apparent in human societies ever since we exchanged hunting and gathering for settled farming. Examples include the medieval European division of society into three 'estates' (nobility, clergy and commoners), and the caste system that has prevailed in Hindu India for at least 2,000 years.

In the caste system, individuals are permanently confined to the caste into which they are born and are forbidden to marry outside their own caste. A person's caste dictates what occupations they may undertake. At the top are the

Brahmin, or priests; and at the very bottom are the Dalits, so-called 'untouchables' who do the most menial work. Although industrialization and government legislation have brought some loosening of the caste system, it is still a powerful force in India.

Under modern industrial capitalism, social divisions are predominantly those of class. The primary determinant of class is economic and as a result there is a greater possibility of social mobility than in the estate or caste systems. Karl Marx (see page 260) conceived of class in terms of a common relationship to capital (property used to generate profit; see page 308), and outlined two main classes: the bourgeoisie, who own most of the capital and employ most of the workforce; and the workers, who do not own capital and work for the bourgeoisie in exchange for wages.

Today we tend to think of class more in terms of status and occupation, an idea first proposed by the German sociologist Max Weber. Such schemes typically place the upper middle class (senior managers and professionals, such as doctors and lawyers) at the top, and unskilled manual workers at the bottom.

Alienation

Alienation is the process by which individuals living under modern industrial capitalism supposedly lose their sense of belonging to society, becoming powerless and depersonalized. Karl Marx (see page 260) maintained that the industrial worker suffers estrangement, reification (in which people become objects) and commodification (where the worker sells him- or herself as a commodity). All these processes arise from the factory system and its division of labour, conditions that lead workers to lose control over their work and become little more than things themselves. The 1936 film *Modern Times* (opposite) starred Charlie Chaplin as a man driven mad by the alienating effects of working on a factory production line.

Some sociologists link alienation with 'anomie', a condition that is prevalent in a society where common beliefs have disintegrated, and moral certainties are absent. Alienation and anomie are both held to lead to unquestioning conformity, political apathy and even psychological difficulties and suicide.

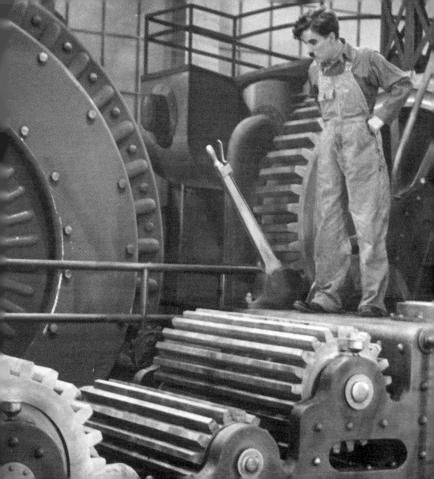

Deviance

Deviance is a term employed by sociologists to denote any departure by an individual from societal norms. Such departures attract the condemnation of the society concerned. 'Norms' are the codes and rules that prevail in a society. Some are based in morality, some are embodied in law, some are purely pragmatic, while others are entirely irrational.

Norms vary from society to society, and shift with time. Even within a society, different groups (such as a particular class or age range) may have their own norms. Some are almost universal – such as taboos against murder, incest and cannibalism. Others are culturally specific – for example, the 'thumbs-up' gesture is interpreted as 'OK' in many European countries, but in southern Sardinia it is a sexual insult.

Societies may consider a whole range of actions, beliefs or conditions to be deviant, from a breach of table manners to a breaking of sexual taboos, from religious disrespect to expressions of racism, from physical or mental disability to serious crimes such as robbery and murder. Condemnations may range from mild disapproval through ostracism to legal sanctions, such as imprisonment or even capital punishment.

Attitudes towards homosexuality over the past few decades illustrate how social norms can change. In the past, psychiatrists regarded homosexuality as not only 'deviant' from 'normal' heterosexuality, but also as a mental illness requiring treatment. At the same time, the law in many Western countries defined it as a crime and punished homosexual acts accordingly. Today, in enlightened societies, homosexuality is regarded as 'different' rather than 'deviant', and has been decriminalized and de-medicalized.

As the creation and defence of social norms is a manifestation of power, some have interpreted any form of deviance as a political act – a refusal to conform to the dictates of the established authority. Such beliefs have been particularly prevalent among left-wing libertarians (see page 254). However, the increased tolerance of many Western societies has taken the subversive edge off many forms of deviance.

Crime

A crime is any act that the law of a country considers to be socially harmful or dangerous. While such acts as theft and murder have been considered crimes in most societies through history, other crimes have been specific to particular societies at particular times. For example, suicide was a crime in the UK until 1961, while 'insider dealing' of stocks and shares only became a crime in many countries in the 1980s.

Crimes can be placed in a number of categories. Crimes against the person include murder and sexual assault; crimes against property include theft and criminal damage; crimes against public order include riot and incitement to racial hatred; and crimes against the state include sedition and treason. In a criminal trial, the prosecution has to establish that the accused committed the offence 'beyond all reasonable doubt', and that he or she fully intended to carry out the act. If found guilty, the accused may be able to plead factors such as self-defence, duress or insanity in mitigation.

Punishment

Crime can be seen as a breach of the rights and freedoms of the victim – including the rights to life and property, and freedom from harm. These are the rights, according to the idea of the social contract (see page 212), that the state exists to uphold. Ironically, the sanction that the state imposes on those who deprive others of such rights and freedoms is often to deny the perpetrators their own rights and freedoms.

There are two main justifications for punishment. The first sees punishment as a good in itself, the expression of justice in which 'the punishment fits the crime'. This retributive view of justice is summed up in the Old Testament edict, 'an eye for an eye, a tooth for a tooth' – a justification that some still resort to today when defending the death penalty for murder.

The imagery of the criminal 'paying' for his or her crime is a common one, and is suggestive of some kind of moral accountancy at work. Once the 'debt to society' is paid off, society supposedly re-achieves balance and stability. In some non-Western countries, the perpetrator of a violent crime may escape punishment by paying 'blood money' to the victim's family, while in some Western countries, the person convicted may be obliged to pay compensation as part of his or her punishment.

The second view of punishment is the utilitarian one (see page 116), which sees punishment not as a good in itself, but as a necessary evil contributing towards the greater good of society. The utilitarian may defend punishment on a range of grounds. One justification holds that depriving criminals of freedom (or even life) prevents them from repeating their crimes, and so keeps society safer. A second maintains that inflicting punishment acts as a deterrent, and therefore dissuades other potential criminals from committing criminal acts, to the common good. The third sees punishment as a way of rehabilitating the criminal for their own benefit, so that he or she may be reintegrated into society.

Psychology

Depending on the practitioner's perspective, psychology can be described as the study of the mind, or of human and animal behaviour, or of the interaction between people and their social and physical environment. Although philosophers have speculated for centuries about the nature of mind, psychology as a separate discipline with aspirations towards scientific objectivity, was only established in 1879 when Wilhelm Wundt (1832–1920) founded a research laboratory in Germany.

Wundt and his contemporaries relied largely on the method of introspection – an attempt to observe and record their own mental processes. However, even Wundt had doubts about his method's reliability, and it was soon eclipsed by behaviourism, which restricts itself to studies of behaviour (see page 364). As the 20th century progressed, numerous other schools of psychology emerged, both theoretical and practical. Among the latter, the fields of educational, clinical and occupational psychology have proved particularly important.

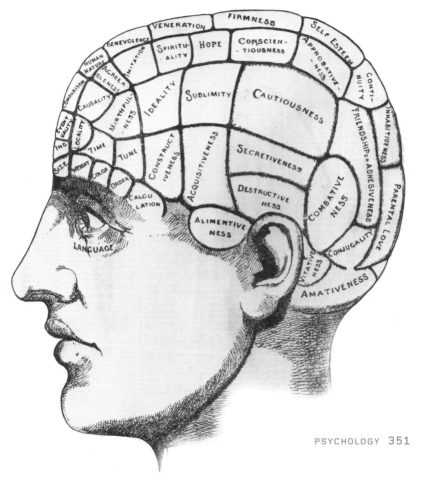

Memory

Memory is at the core of our sense of personal identity (see page 38). It is also essential to our functioning as intelligent beings. Without memory we would have no notion of having a past, no concept of our own relationship with others or with the external world. And without memory we would not retain any data or knowledge or experience on which to base our present and future actions.

Memory consists of three processes: registration, by which an experience is logged in the mind; retention, by which it is held in the mind (over what may be a short or a long period); and recall, by which the experience is brought out of storage and to our attention.

Every day, our senses are subjected to vast inputs of data from the external world, but only a very small proportion of this is registered. Our brains have learnt to select what is important. Retention requires a degree of repetition – for example, to learn a poem off by heart, we have to recite it again and again, and to retain an image of a place, we repeatedly summon it up in our 'mind's eye'.

Recall depends on some kind of cue, usually involving association. Famously, the French novelist Marcel Proust found a gateway into the 'lost time' of his earlier life when he tasted a madeleine cake dipped in a cup of tea, as he had done as a boy – the inspiration for his novel sequence *À la recherche du temps perdu*.

Neurophysiologists are beginning to understand how memory relates to physical processes within the human brain. The brain consists of billions of nerve cells or neurones, each capable of transmitting nerve impulses electrochemically to other neurones. It is thought that as we register experiences, certain patterns of connection are made in particular groups of neurones. It is possible that memories are retained when such connections become well-worn pathways and recalled when some stimulus activates that pathway.

Perception and sensation

It is usual to distinguish between sensation and perception. Sensation denotes the process by which our senses – such as sight, hearing, touch, smell and taste – register inputs from the outside world and send them to the brain. Perception denotes how we perceive or experience the inputs supplied by sensation, and involves a degree of interpretation, often based on previous experiences and the mental map these have enabled us to make of the world.

To illustrate the difference between sensation and perception, take the example of a young baby. Its eyes register the same data as those of an adult, but – because it has no idea of what it is looking at – its perception is entirely different. With experience, perception enables us to make predictions – for example, to assume the whole of an object is present, even when we can only see part of it. It may also lead us into error, as is the case with optical illusions.

Most people perceive this simple drawing either as a beautiful young girl or an ugly old crone. Whichever image is perceived first, it will be suddenly replaced by the other.

Intelligence

The question of what constitutes intelligence is one that continues to excite considerable debate, as do questions over whether genetic inheritance or environment play the dominant role in determining an individual's intelligence.

In the early years of the 20th century the French psychologist Alfred Binet (1857–1911) developed the first intelligence tests, which he applied to schoolchildren. Soon afterwards, a statistical basis for such tests was supplied in the form of 'intelligence quotient' or IQ, which is based on the ratio of actual to mental age, the latter being derived from the test results. IQ tests typically use both verbal and non-verbal reasoning, and supposedly measure innate intelligence. However, this claim has been undermined by the fact that children can be taught how to do better at IQ tests.

A different model of intelligence was suggested by Swiss psychologist Jean Piaget (1896–1980). Piaget studied thought processes in children, particularly perception, judgement and reasoning, and described a series of qualitatively different stages in the development of adult intelligence. He concluded that this development depends on environmental factors to provide the necessary experiences, and that children's education should be tailored towards enhancing this process.

Neither IQ tests nor Piaget's model take account of cultural differences. A third approach sees intelligence as culturally defined: societies value certain skills over others. For example, hunter-gatherers value knowledge of the natural environment and the ability to combine this with practical skills such as tracking and hunting. The skills required to do well in IQ tests, while perhaps valuable in modern industrial societies, would be largely irrelevant to them.

Another approach emphasizes the importance of 'emotional intelligence'. Advocates of this approach suggest that cognitive aspects of intelligence such as problem-solving are only part of the story. Of equal importance to our successful functioning, they suggest, is the ability to understand and control one's own emotions and those of others.

Emotion

An emotion is any strong feeling, such as anger, fear, joy or sorrow. Emotions are not just internal phenomena, and are often manifested in behaviour, such as facial expressions. Darwin noted that the ability to recognize the significance of expressions is important to survival.

Emotions involve a complex mixture of environmental input, subjective experience, physiological changes and behavioural output. For example, the perception of danger induces a feeling of fear and a burst of the hormone adrenaline, which increases heart rate and the level of glucose in the blood – changes that prepare the subject for 'fight or flight'. To take another example, depression is often accompanied by a reduced level of the chemical serotonin in the body. But whether it is external factors (such as unemployment or bereavement) that have caused the feelings of depression, or the changes in body chemistry, is impossible to say. Mechanistic explanations can only ever be part of the story.

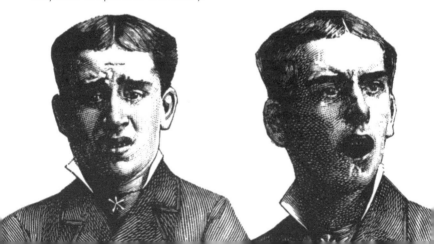

Psychoanalysis and Freudianism

The Austrian psychiatrist Sigmund Freud (1856–1939) was one of the most influential figures of the 20th century. Although many of his theories have since been dismissed as unscientific, his ideas about the unconscious and the centrality of sex in human experience have fundamentally altered the way that people think about themselves.

In Vienna in the late 19th century, Freud pioneered the theory known as psychoanalysis, by which means he treated patients with a variety of neuroses, such as hysteria. Freud believed that neuroses are caused by the repression of childhood experiences, which are nevertheless stored in the unconscious. He maintained that by using a 'talking cure', involving free association of ideas on the part of the patient and an exploration of the patient's dreams, the unconscious could be opened up and repressed memories brought into the open.

Freud suggested that the mind has three components. The selfish, instinctual part that demands pleasure and satisfaction he called the id. The ego is the conscious mind, which has to deal with the conflicting demands of the id and the superego – the latter being the Freudian equivalent of conscience, which generates feelings of guilt. More shockingly at the time, Freud also proposed that human sexuality commences in infancy, not at puberty as previously believed. For example, he originated the idea of the Oedipus complex, in which boys of three to six years old unconsciously want to have sex with their mothers and kill their fathers. Freud believed that the repression of childhood sexuality resulted in neuroses and unhappiness in later life.

Scientists today criticize Freud's theories on the grounds that they are untestable. It is not possible to prove the existence of the unconscious as Freud conceived it, let alone to demonstrate that repressed desires motivate behaviour as Freud maintained. It is also not possible to establish whether the success a psychoanalyst achieves with a patient is due to the theory or to the personality of the psychoanalyst.

Conditioning and conditioned reflexes

Conditioning is the process by which behaviour can be modified by changing the stimuli associated with it, and thus changing the response. Classical conditioning was pioneered by the Russian physiologist Ivan Pavlov (1849–1936), who, in a famous series of experiments, showed that the presence of food causes dogs to salivate. If the appearance of food is systematically accompanied by the ringing of a bell, in due course the dogs will salivate on hearing the bell, even when food is not present. This is called a conditioned reflex.

The other main form of conditioning is operant conditioning. Whereas classical conditioning involves a part of the nervous system beyond conscious control, operant conditioning seeks to alter voluntary behaviour by means of rewards and punishments, a process called reinforcement. Such techniques have been used by psychiatrists in aversion therapy, and by educational and industrial psychologists. Both kinds of conditioning are of interest to behaviourists (see page 364).

Behaviourism

Behaviourism is a school of psychology that dominated the field for the first half of the 20th century. One of its earliest proponents was the American psychologist J.B. Watson (1878–1958), who rejected introspection – the methodology that had previously prevailed – as hopelessly subjective. Instead, he proposed that psychology, to be counted as a science, should restrict itself to observations of behaviour and eschew all speculations about inner states, such as thoughts, ideas and feelings.

To this end, behaviourists in many countries set up laboratory experiments, involving both humans and animals, in order to study various forms of behaviour, and particularly those that could be measured. Such experiments were largely restricted to providing a stimulus and observing the response, then statistically analysing the results to discover what laws might relate the two.

Soviet physiologist Ivan Pavlov's groundbreaking experiments with dogs established the principles of classical conditioning (see page 362). In America, behaviourist B.F. Skinner (1904–90), applied the methodology of stimulus and response to develop the principles of operant conditioning. Skinner devised the 'Skinner box' to standardize the teaching of simple actions to animals such as rats and pigeons, and went on to extend his approach to look at human behaviour, devising various educational aids. Some psychiatrists adopted operant conditioning to treat humans with various behaviour disorders, using rewards and punishments to teach new behaviours, and to eradicate behaviour regarded as undesirable.

However, behaviourism has been criticized as overly deterministic and reductionist, addressing only superficial aspects of behaviour in contrived conditions. Behaviourism disregards the factor of conscious choice, and appears unable to address complex phenomena such as emotion, language and relationships. Although it provides many insights into animal behaviour, in human psychology it has largely been superseded by the cognitive approach (see page 368).

Evolutionary psychology

Evolutionary psychology seeks to explain psychological traits as adaptations due to either natural or sexual selection (see page 196). Proponents believe that much human behaviour has evolved in the same way as our physical characteristics – as a way of dealing with common problems that faced our ancestors. Evolutionary psychology downplays the role of culture, although it does not eliminate it entirely. For example, the universal human ability to use language is said to be an evolutionary adaptation, while specific languages are cultural constructs. Other examples of adaptation commonly cited by evolutionary psychologists include altruism, kin-recognition, cooperation, male aggression and mate selection.

The hypotheses of evolutionary psychology have been criticized as untestable. However, a number of hypotheses *have* been successfully tested: for example, humans have been shown to remember content relevant to survival (e.g. food, predators, shelter) much more readily than content that is irrelevant.

Cognitive theory

The term 'cognitive psychology' was coined by the American psychologist Ulric Neisser in his 1965 book of the same name. As a field it is concerned with cognition, a term that embraces all psychological processes involved in acquiring, organizing and using knowledge, from the analysis of sensory stimuli to the ordering of subjective experience.

Like behaviourism (see page 364), cognitive psychology rejects introspection for scientific method. But unlike behaviourism, it acknowledges the existence of internal mental states, studying such processes as perception, memory, thought, language and problem-solving. Its acceptance of internal mental states was initially criticized as lacking empirical support, but neuroscience has subsequently provided evidence that mental states correlate with physiological brain states.

Underlying cognitive psychology is the conception of humans as 'dynamic information-processing systems', analogous to computers. Neisser stated that cognition embraces 'all processes by which the sensory input is transformed, reduced, elaborated, stored, recovered, and used. It is concerned with these processes even when they operate in the absence of relevant stimulation, as in images and hallucinations ...' Advances in artificial intelligence (see page 192) in the 1960s and 1970s contributed to developments in cognitive psychology, and both – together with neuroscience (the study of the brain and the nervous system) – are often seen as branches of a new interdisciplinary field, cognitive science.

Cognitive psychology has many practical applications. Cognitive behavioural therapy (CBT), for example, draws on both cognitive and behaviourist theory, particularly operant conditioning (see page 362). Like psychoanalysis (see page 360), CBT is a 'talking cure', but rather than delving into the past to uncover the causes of present maladies, CBT concentrates on the here and now. Using various goal-oriented systematic procedures, CBT aims to address a range of dysfunctional emotions, behaviours and cognitions, and has been shown to be effective in many cases of clinical depression, bulimia, obsessive-compulsive disorder and post-traumatic stress disorder.

Psychometrics

Psychometrics is the branch of psychology that seeks to measure phenomena such as intelligence, knowledge, abilities, attitudes and personality traits. Systematic mental testing was initiated in the late 19th century by the English scientist Francis Galton (1822–1911) in his studies of heredity. Subsequently, much work was put into measuring intelligence using standardized IQ tests (see page 356). Such tests have been used extensively for educational and vocational selection, though they have been criticized for cultural bias.

Over recent decades, human resources departments have increasingly used psychometric testing to screen potential employees. Tests seek to establish aptitudes, attitudes and 'personality type', and often take the form of a long series of multiple-choice questions asking how the subject would respond in various situations. Supporters claim these tests give them an accurate picture of a candidate's suitabillity for a job. Critics claim there is little scientific basis for this view.

In the Rorschach inkblot test, subjects are shown a
number of cards with apparently random patterns
on them and asked what they see. Their responses
supposedly give clues to their character.

Art

Art embraces not only the visual arts, but also literature, music, dance and cinema. What is it that links these varied activities? And do they have a function beyond mere entertainment, or are they just the icing on top of life's cake, pleasurable but not essential?

All the arts involve formal structures, from the arrangement of shapes in a painting to the sequence of shots in a film, and from the rhyme scheme of a sonnet to the pattern of themes in a symphonic movement. Such formal structures present a kind of language, a series of conventions that both the creator and the audience are familiar with, and within the framework of these conventions the creator may attempt to engage one or more of the senses and stimulate the emotions and intellect of the audience.

For many centuries, artists were regarded as no more than highly skilled craftsmen, and what they produced was often valued primarily for the function it had. Although in ancient Greece the creation of beauty was treasured for its own sake, in medieval Europe much art served a religious purpose. Paintings of the Holy Family and the saints provided a focus for piety, while much music had a liturgical function, and the finest buildings were the great cathedrals.

The idea that there was some separate and special human activity called art began to re-emerge in the Renaissance and became firmly established with the Romantic movement (see page 386). The Romantics insisted upon the special role of the artist, a lonely figure who stood apart from society, and who through inspiration, genius and struggle created works that had the capacity to transform humanity.

Today, although our capacity to be moved by works of art remains unchanged, we are more likely to see artists as products of their period, class and culture, whose values are embodied in their art. Gone are the god-like figures who gave us glimpses of higher realms of being.

Mimesis

Mimesis is an ancient Greek word that has been variously translated as 'representation' or 'imitation', and denotes the process by which art is said to 'hold a mirror up to nature'. When Aristotle (see page 16) used the term, he suggested that art actually improves upon nature. The real world is full of incidentals and trivialities; what art does is to select and structure the most significant material from that world in order to give voice to higher truths.

How 'true' is art? A painting is not the thing it represents, a novel is, by definition, 'fiction'. Should we therefore dismiss all art as 'lies'? This would almost certainly be to commit what the philosophers call a category error (see page 90). We view and interpret the world through all kinds of mental constructs (language, religious belief and the scientific method, to name but a few). Art is just one of such lenses, but one that often helps us to see more clearly.

Imagery

One of the key components of literature, as well as the visual arts, is imagery. In the visual arts, imagery takes the form of depictions of things, while in literature the writer may use words to evoke mental pictures, or to evoke other sensory experiences, such as sounds and smells. Such imagery may be deployed to conjure up a scene; or it may create a new perspective on something familiar; or it may point to or suggest additional, non-literal, layers of meaning, as is the case with allegory (see page 378) and symbolism (see page 392).

In literature, the two most basic rhetorical devices involving imagery are simile and metaphor. Simile is when something is compared to something else – for example, 'My love is like a red, red rose'. Metaphor is when something is said to *be* something else – for example, 'Go, lovely rose!' Both have a similar effect of associating one thing with another and thereby intensifying, refreshing or complicating our perception of it.

Some images may turn into literary conventions. For example, in Homer's epics, the sea is always 'wine-dark' and dawn 'rosy-fingered', while in Anglo-Saxon poetry the sea is often the 'whale way' and a river the 'swan way'.

Medieval and Renaissance literature and painting is full of standard images, religious or otherwise, which the audience would understand. For example, the Holy Spirit is depicted as a white dove and the pelican symbolizes self-sacrificial parental devotion (from the belief that it pecks its own breast to feed its young on its blood), while the eagle represents imperial power.

Creative artists often like to play with conventional imagery, just as they like to subvert expectations provided by other artistic conventions. Hence when Shakespeare begins Sonnet 18 by asking 'Shall I compare thee to a summer's day?' we are surprised to hear that the beloved is *not* like a summer's day, but is in fact something even better. And when he begins Sonnet 130 with 'My mistress' eyes are nothing like the sun', we know the old clichés are about to be refreshed, if not flushed away entirely.

Allegory

An allegory is a piece of literature or visual art in which the components – such as characters, objects and places – systematically stand for other things, so that an apparently simple story or painting in fact carries a body of additional meaning. The intent may be didactic, moral or satirical.

Allegories often involve personifications of abstractions, for example Bronzino's painting *An Allegory of Venus and Cupid* (*c*.1545) contains a number of figures, thought to stand for Folly, Fraud, Jealousy and Time (opposite). An example of a less problematic allegory is John Bunyan's *Pilgrim's Progress* (1678), which recounts the journey of the hero, Christian, from the City of Destruction through such places as Vanity Fair and the Slough of Despond to his final destination, the Celestial City. A notable modern allegory is George Orwell's *Animal Farm* (1945), a fable that presents an unambiguous critique of how revolutionary idealism in Russia became corrupted under Stalin – represented in the novel by a pig called Napoleon.

The novel

For some 300 years, the novel has been the dominant literary form. Prior to this, poetry – particularly epic poetry – held pride of place. Epics such as Homer's *Iliad*, Virgil's *Aeneid* and Milton's *Paradise Lost* dealt with grand themes, often drawn from myth or scripture and involving gods and heroes. In contrast, the novel predominantly (though not exclusively) presents a recognizable, everyday world, with characters who, although fictional, lead lives not far removed from those of the reader.

Prose fiction existed in the ancient world, for example the *Satyricon* of the Roman writer Petronius. In the Middle Ages and the Renaissance, prose tales, fables and romances were popular among the literate minority. It is the pretensions and fantasies of the romances, with their stories of distressed maidens and chivalrous knights, that are satirized in what is generally recognized as the first true novel, *Don Quixote* (1605, 1615), by Spanish writer Miguel de Cervantes. The tension between the knightly delusions of the elderly Don Quixote and the reality of the modern world he lives in provides considerable pathos.

The popularity of the novel increased exponentially in the 18th century, assisted by the spread of literacy. Writers adopted a range of techniques and approaches. Some sought to add to verisimilitude by using a first-person narrator, such as the title character in Daniel Defoe's *Robinson Crusoe* (1719), which thus reads like an autobiography. Others developed the epistolary novel, in which the story is presented in a series of letters – Samuel Richardson's *Clarissa* (1747–8) is a famous example.

A range of genres emerged, from Gothic horror to historical romance, but during the 19th century the novel came to be predominantly realist (see page 388), presenting a cross-section of contemporary society, while at the same time paying attention to individual character development and the intricacies of plot. The advent of Modernism (see page 396) in the early 20th century saw many of the conventions of the novel overthrown – although this fever for experimentation has proved to be a somewhat transient phenomenon.

The Baroque

The word 'Baroque' was applied by later critics to the style that dominated art and architecture in Europe in the 17th and early 18th centuries. The term derives from *barroco*, the Portuguese word for a rough or imperfectly shaped pearl. The label was intended as derogatory, referring to the asymmetry, ornamentation, dramatic chiaroscuro (contrasts of light and shade) and extravagance of the style, in contrast to the calm and balance of Renaissance art. The Baroque was primarily a vehicle for the Counter-Reformation, the Catholic Church's vigorous response to the spread of Protestantism. It sought to convey power and emotional intensity, qualities epitomized in the sculptures of Bernini, the paintings of Caravaggio and Rubens, and in churches from Bavaria to Latin America.

The application of the label Baroque to the music of the same period is somewhat arbitrary, although the term perhaps suits the ornateness of some styles. Among the leading Baroque composers were Monteverdi, Vivaldi and J.S. Bach.

Classicism

Classicism is a broad tendency within the arts that seeks to perpetuate the aesthetic values of classical Greece (c.500–338 BC). These values are often characterized as balance, proportion, reason and harmony, qualities held to embody both an idealized beauty and an orderly serenity.

The visual arts of classical Greek that have proved the most enduring are its architecture and sculpture. Greek architecture is based on geometrical shapes – the circle, the square, the triangle and the rectangle. The 'orders' of Greek architecture, Doric, Ionic and Corinthian (most readily seen in the decorative style at the top of pillars), have given many later architects a vocabulary on which to base their own designs. In sculpture, the Greeks set out to idealize the human face and figure, rather than representing individuals, with all their peculiar features and flaws – echoing Plato's theory of the Forms (see page 14).

The Romans borrowed extensively from Greek art, but after the fall of Rome in the 5th century AD, classical values fell into the shadows for a thousand years, until revived in the Renaissance, when artists and architects enthusiastically embraced Greek and Roman forms. In architecture particularly, classicism has remained enormously influential.

In literature, too, the models of the ancient Greeks and Romans were revived at the Renaissance, when critics developed Aristotle's writings on drama (see pages 126–7) into the idea of the three unities – of action, place and time. These rules were strictly observed by the great 17th-century French dramatists Racine and Corneille; but William Shakespeare (1564–1616), a far greater playwright, paid no attention to the rules and was thus condemned at this time as an uncouth barbarian.

The 'classical' period in music (c.1770–1820) – the era of Haydn, Mozart and Beethoven – owes less to the productions of classical Greece, although the emphasis on balanced structure and harmonious resolution are certainly classical in spirit.

Romanticism

The Romantic movement that swept through Europe and America from the later 18th century partly defined itself as the antithesis of classicism (see page 384). Classical values of calm and reason were rejected in favour of struggle and passion. The artist, far from being a pillar of an ordered society, became a lonely, inspired genius at odds with the rest of the world. Beauty no longer resided in well-manicured landscapes, but in wilderness and the violence of the elements.

The first stirrings of Romanticism came with the German literary movement known as *Sturm und Drang* ('storm and stress'). Writers such as Goethe (1749–1832) and Schiller (1759–1805) led the way, followed by many writers in other countries, from Wordsworth and Shelley to Victor Hugo and Alexander Pushkin. The spirit of Romanticism also infected idealist philosophers such as Kant and Hegel (see page 63), and painters and composers from Turner to Tchaikovsky.

Wanderer Above the Sea of Fog, painted in 1818
by Caspar David Friedrich

Realism and naturalism

In literature and the visual arts, realism describes an approach in which the artist attempts to depict the world as it is, rather than some idealized or imaginary world. The term is particularly associated with the post-Romantic period, when realists rejected the sentimentalism and idealization of much 18th-century literature and art, and also the subjectivity, emotionalism and obsession with grand and heroic subjects that marked the Romantics.

The term 'realism' was first used in France in the 1830s in reference to the novelists Balzac and Stendhal. In his great sequence of novels and stories begun in 1835 and collectively known as *La Comédie Humaine* ('The Human Comedy'), Balzac shines an unflinching light on the French society of his own time. Balzac's characters are complex human beings, morally neither black nor white, but painted in various shades of grey. Balzac's focus on contemporary (or near-contemporary) society and his psychologically perceptive characterization is shared by other realist writers, from Flaubert and Maupassant in France to Turgenev, Gogol, Tolstoy and Chekhov in Russia, and Dickens, Trollope and George Eliot in England.

In art, realism also originated in France, where raw and unsentimental scenes from contemporary life, such as Courbet's *The Stonebreakers* (1850) and Manet's *Le Déjeuner sur l'herbe* (1863) – depicting two prostitutes with their clients – scandalized the public. In landscape painting, too, the *plein air* practice of painters such as Corot and Théodore Rousseau, whereby paintings were executed in the open air rather than in the studio, also proved controversial.

Towards the end of the 19th century, a new literary approach appeared: naturalism. Where realist novels are selective in what they choose to describe, and often focus on a few individuals, the naturalist novels of writers such as Zola in France, Gorki in Russia and Dreiser in the USA contain swathes of 'scientific' social observation and are more concerned with how social environments determine the ways in which people as a whole behave, and how society might be reformed.

Impressionism

Impressionism was an art movement that originated in France in the 1860s. It took its name from a painting exhibited by Claude Monet at the first Impressionist exhibition in 1874: *Impression: Sunrise*. Among the other Impressionists were Renoir, Manet, Degas, Pissarro, Cézanne, Mary Cassatt, Sisley, Seurat and Signac, while Cézanne, Gauguin and Van Gogh are often labelled Post-Impressionists. Like the realists before them (see page 389), the Impressionists concentrated on scenes from modern life and painted landscapes *en plein air*.

The Impressionists were responsible for many innovations. They sought to capture transient 'impressions' of light and movement, rejecting hard outlines, adopting unusual perspectives and experimenting with beushwork to see what effects could be created by juxtaposing different colours and textures. Their impact on art was profound. For example, Van Gogh influenced the Expressionists, Cézanne the Cubists, and Monet the Abstract Expressionists.

Symbolism

It is common to distinguish between symbols and signs, both forms of imagery (see page 376) used in art and literature. Allegories (see page 378) and fables are generally systems of signs, in which there is usually a simple one-to-one relationship between signifier and signified, a bit like translating from one language into another. So 'Cupid' stands for 'love', while 'Mr Fox' denotes 'cunning'.

Symbols work in less straightforward ways, combining denotation with connotation, the latter being the process by which a word, phrase, object or picture suggests a range of associations or ideas.

For example, the title 'character' in Herman Melville's novel *Moby-Dick* (1851) is not simply a great white whale. As the tale unfolds, the whale accumulates a mass of symbolic roles – it becomes the epitome of evil, the God whom man wishes to destroy, the untameable otherness and indifference of the universe, the object of man's questing ambitions. It even comes to embody the folly of searching for meaning where none exists.

Symbols such as the white whale can thus yield great riches, but their ambiguities can also verge on mystification. This has certainly been a criticism levelled at the Symbolist movement that arose in France in the later 19th century, partly as a reaction to realism (see page 388). Symbolist poets such as Paul Verlaine and Stéphane Mallarmé explored the musical and associative qualities of language to suggest evanescent emotions and uncertain states of being, shimmering on the borders of the physical and spiritual worlds.

There was also a Symbolist movement in painting, in which the key figures were Odilon Redon and Gustave Moreau. Of greater significance was the impact the Symbolist poets had on the great Modernist writers, including T.S. Eliot, Ezra Pound, W.B. Yeats, James Joyce and Rainer Maria Rilke.

Aestheticism

In 1818, the French philosopher Victor Cousin gave a lecture to the Sorbonne in Paris, in which he stated: 'We must have religion for religion's sake, morality for morality's sake, as with art for art's sake ... the beautiful cannot be the way to what is useful, or to what is good, or to what is holy; it leads only to itself.'

The phrase 'art for art's sake' became the slogan of aestheticism, a tendency prominent in the 19th century that rejected the notion that art should serve any purpose other than itself, and placed the artist in an 'ivory tower'. Aestheticism was embraced by various groups, such as the Symbolists, the Pre-Raphaelites and the Aesthetic movement. The most notable proponent of the latter was Oscar Wilde, who famously wrote 'It is better to be beautiful than to be good.' Such epigrams, in highlighting the elitism, affectations and amorality of aestheticism, ironically helped to undermine the seriousness of art itself.

One of Aubrey Beardsley's illustrations for Oscar Wilde's play *Salome* (1896)

Modernism and Postmodernism

Modernism was the great artistic project of the 20th century. The aim of Modernism, whether stated or not, was immensely serious – to transform the way that we perceive and think of the world and of ourselves. To do this, the arid old conventions were dynamited to create a completely new start, a 'ground zero' upon which the bold and the visionary could experiment with new conceptions of art and reality. As a consequence, much of the new art that the Modernists created was deliberately challenging and 'difficult'.

Modernist ambitions stirred up all the arts. In music, conventional tonality was abandoned by composers such as Schoenberg, Stravinsky and Bartók, and there were also experiments with new colours, rhythms and structures. In the visual arts, the idea that the painting presents a 'window onto the world' through the picture-plane gave way to the multiple perspectives of Cubism (see page 402), the formalist values of abstraction (see page 400), the emotional intensity of

Expressionism (see page 398) and the Surrealists' explorations of the unconscious (see page 404).

In literature, the fragmentation of syntax, subject-matter and viewpoint begun by the Symbolists (see page 393) was taken to greater extremes. T.S. Eliot's poem *The Waste Land* (1922), for example, comprises a collage of scenes, voices and images that form a poetic counterpart to the physical, moral and spiritual desolation left by the First World War. James Joyce's novel *Ulysses* (1922) was similarly innovative, replacing linear narrative with multiple viewpoints and unedited 'streams of consciousness', representing the immediate thoughts and sensations of the characters.

Towards the end of the 20th century, critics began to apply the adjective 'Postmodern' to works of art that drew on the new conventions established by Modernism, but in a self-referential and often playful way that replaced the heroic ambitions of the Modernists with a knowing, ironic self-consciousness – as found, for example, in the fictions of Vladimir Nabokov, Kurt Vonnegut or Jorge Luis Borges.

Expressionism

I n 1907 the Norwegian painter Edvard Munch wrote that 'A work of art can come only from the interior of man.' This could be the slogan of Expressionism, an artistic movement of the early 20th century characterized by boldness, distortion and exaggeration, in which, according to the painter Oskar Kokoschka, 'the image becomes the embodiment of the soul'.

Expressionism was particularly strong in Germany and Austria, and became even darker in the wake of the First World War, as can be seen in the nightmare visions of Max Beckmann and the savage satires of George Grosz. Expressionism also infused the other arts – for example, the earlier music of Schoenberg, the plays of Strindberg and Wedekind, and German silent cinema. A notable example of the latter is Robert Weine's 1919 film *The Cabinet of Dr Caligari* (opposite), in which the crazy angles of the sets, the strong contrasts of light and shade, and the focus on heightened states of emotion and madness are all typical of the movement.

Abstraction

The invention of photography in the 19th century rendered the strictly representational purpose of painting – 'to hold a mirror up to nature' – redundant. Some artists turned to Expressionism (see page 398), while others indulged in formal experimentation. Among the latter, some – such as the Cubists (see page 402) – sought to reduce the appearance of objects to simplified forms. The results may appear abstract, but true abstraction rejects any type of representation, instead building the work of art out of non-representational forms – ranging from sharply delineated geometrical shapes to wild brushstrokes or even splashes of paint.

The first truly abstract paintings were made around 1910–11 in Bavaria by the Russian painter Wassily Kandinsky. 'If in a picture a line is freed from the aim of designating a thing and functions as a thing itself,' Kandinsky wrote in 1912, 'its inner resonance is not weakened by any subordinate roles and acquires its full inner strength.' Kandinsky drew analogies between abstract painting and music, that most abstract of the arts, and emphasized its spiritual dimension.

The Dutch artist Piet Mondrian, whose paintings typically consist of black grid lines on a white ground, with one or two squares or rectangles picked out in a primary colour, took a similarly spiritual view. In 1937 he wrote that 'Abstract art … is opposed to the raw primitive animal nature of man, but it is one with true human nature.'

Painters such as Mondrian represent the purest, most minimalist type of geometrical abstraction. In contrast, the form of abstract painting that erupted in the USA in the years after the Second World War was an altogether wilder, looser and more heroic affair, which became known as Abstract Expressionism. Some Abstract Expressionists, such as Jackson Pollock, developed the technique known as action painting, in which pots of paint were flung across the canvas in acts of spontaneous creation.

Although going in and out of fashion, both geometric and 'free' abstraction have continued as major strands in modern art.

Cubism

The Post-Impressionist painter Paul Cézanne (1839–1906) increasingly sought to draw out the structures lying within natural objects and landscapes. In 1904 he laid out his credo: 'Treat nature in terms of the cylinder, the sphere, the cone.' Cézanne's approach, rejecting the surface sensuousness of the Impressionists in favour a more classical concern with form, had a profound effect on a young Spanish artist called Pablo Picasso (1881–1973), who around 1907, alongside French painter Georges Braque, originated a new movement: Cubism.

Cubists often experimented with still life, restricting the colour range and ignoring light effects in order to concentrate on form. Traditional perspective, with its single viewpoint and illusionistic ambition, was replaced by multiple viewpoints, in which objects were represented from different angles, then put together as overlapping or interlocking elements. This new way of representing solidity and volume on a two-dimensional plane was to have a lasting influence on 20th-century painting.

Surrealism

The writings of Sigmund Freud (see page 360) on dreams, repressed desires and the unconsciousness opened up a whole new world to artists and writers. The breaking of old taboos – especially those barring the discussion of sex – and the recognition of the irrational in human nature was to many a liberating experience. It was also revolutionary in its potential for bringing traditional conservative values crashing down. The painters, playwrights and poets of the Surrealist movement of the 1920s and 1930s were at the forefront of this effort to subvert bourgeois conventionality.

The iconoclastic tendency in modern art was not completely new. Before the First World War the Futurists in Italy had rejected all earlier art and held the motor car to be the epitome of beauty, while during the war the Dada movement similarly renounced existing aesthetic values. One leading Dadaist, Marcel Duchamp (1887–1968), famously displayed a urinal in an art gallery, giving it the title *Fountain* (1917).

Surrealism emerged directly from Dada on the latter's demise in 1922. The chief spokesman of the new movement, André Breton (1896–1966), defined Surrealism as 'pure psychic automatism, by which it is intended to express, whether verbally or in writing, or in any other way, the real process of thought. Thought's dictation, free from any control by the reason, independent of aesthetic or moral preoccupation.' Breton aligned the Surrealists with communism, although the Communist Party declined to reciprocate.

Following Breton's urging, much Surrealist literature was based on automatic writing – scribbling down whatever came into one's head. Some Surrealist artists followed similar procedures (for example, Max Ernst's *frottages* and André Masson's free ink drawings), or assembled artworks from randomly 'found' objects. Others such as Salvador Dali and René Magritte created dreamlike worlds out of bizarrely juxtaposed objects. Such tableaux were also incorporated into theatre pieces and films. After the Second World War, however, Surrealism largely lost its power to shock and became absorbed into the commercial mainstream.

Structuralism and Poststructuralism

Structuralism is a mode of critical analysis that arose from linguistics in the 1950s and spread across the arts, anthropology and psychology. Its basic premise is that all cultural phenomena consist of systems of verbal and non-verbal signs. The signs alone are meaningless – instead, meaning arises from their relationships, which are often binary oppositions such as nature/culture, male/female, and active/passive. For example, the theorist Roland Barthes suggested that wrestlers signify the hero/villain opposition. Such systems comprise a 'language', and the human mind, rather than being a creator of these languages, is in fact determined by them.

Structuralists maintain that such languages are open to scientific study, while post-structuralists hold that language is evasive and unstable, and meanings merely provisional. They are sceptical about the explanatory validity of activities such as philosophy and history, arguing that these too are languages, and thus just as evasive as their subject matter.

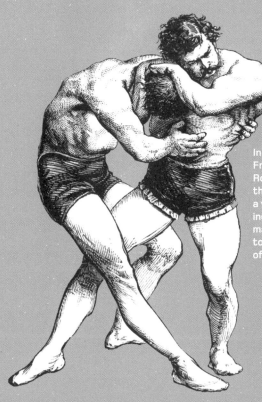

In *Mythologies* (1957), the French literary theorist Roland Barthes analysed the cultural language of a variety of phenomena, including wrestling matches, which he likened to the formalized theatre of classical Greece.

Index

Quercus Publishing Plc

21 Bloomsbury Square

London

WC1A 2NS

First published in 2011

A catalogue record of this book is available from
the British Library

UK and associated territories
    Hardback edition: 978 0 85738 618 2
    Paperback edition: 978 1 78087 145 5

US and associated territories: 978 1 84866 159 2

Printed and bound in China

10 9 8 7 6 5 4 3 2 1